BUILD A BETTER BOND:

100+ Ways To Connect With Your Horse

Suzannah Kolbeck

HoneyFern Press

BALTIMORE, MARYLAND

Cover Design by Kim Mattison

Cover photography by Fred Moon

HoneyFern Press
Baltimore, MD 21211

Publisher's Note: This book provides general information about horse training and riding based on the author's experiences and expertise. However, each horse and rider is unique and may respond differently to these practices. The author and publisher disclaim responsibility for any injuries or damages that may occur from applying these methods. Always prioritize safety and consider professional supervision, especially if you're a beginner or dealing with challenging horses. Despite our efforts for accuracy, errors may persist. We assume no liability for any risk or loss resulting from the use of this book. Always consult with a professional horse trainer or an equine veterinarian before implementing significant changes in your horse's routine or care.

Build A Better Bond: 100+ Ways To Connect With Your Horse / Suzannah Kolbeck.
First Edition.
ISBN: 9798865956228

For Sadie Mae and all of the other equine teachers who have helped me become a better person.

"Fascination with horses predated every other single thing I knew. Before I was a mother, before I was a writer, before I knew the facts of life, before I was a schoolgirl, before I learned to read, I wanted a horse."

Jane Smiley

CONTENTS

INTRODUCTION

"I'm still on the move, I'm getting better because I'm still studying. I still want to be a better horseman." Buck Brannaman

There is no arguing this one simple fact: horses are magical creatures. With flowing manes and tails and sleek bodies designed to split the wind, horses are mesmerizing and magnificent.

Not only are they magical, but they do something for humans that is practically unthinkable in the natural world. They ignore thousands of years of evolution and instinct and allow people to strap the hide of a dead animal on their back, get on top of that hide, and manipulate their heads with a cold piece of metal between their teeth.

Horses do this even though some humans are cruel, impatient, and occasionally abusive. They forgive our many faults, even when they are in pain and scared. Their hearts are enormous; horses offer them up, even when their instincts scream for them to run away. They submit, perhaps, because they often have no choice. But it doesn't have to be this way. Working with your horse doesn't need to be a contest of wills with one submitting to the other. It can instead be a dance, an equal partnership, with everyone's need for safety, security, and connection fulfilled.

This understanding of the importance of connection—vaquero horsemen refer to this as *feel,* when a horse reaches for you as you reach for them—is not new in the horse world, but many horse owners both novice and experienced struggle to find a way in with their horse. For experienced riders, it may be coming across a horse that isn't responding to your usual way of doing things. For new owners, it might be figuring out where to begin.

Love of and passion for horses is a great start, but they don't directly translate into a genuine working partnership. This foundation may crack and crumble when a horse and rider pair are confronted with a new situation or come up against a training obstacle.

My story in horses began with an unplanned dismount at the age of five on a docile trail horse spooked by a shadow, and it continued intermittently throughout adolescence and early adulthood. The main feature of this tale is that I fell off every horse I ever rode until the age of 17 when I put away the idea of horses for the practical task of college and figuring out exactly what I would be doing with my life. With the exception of my continuing education in horses via videos, books, and magazines, my only hands-on experience came on vacation-rented trail ponies with checked-out eyes and a deep desire to just get through the day.

That all changed when I turned 31. Without anyone to guide me, I decided to re-introduce horses into my life. I figured the best way to do that was to make myself useful in a barn, so I began volunteering every Saturday at a horse rescue, feeding 100 horses and mucking 25 stalls, rain or shine, for three years. Living in the suburbs of Marietta, Georgia, with a four-year-old at home and a full-time job teaching middle school, this was the closest I could get to horses, and it was (mostly) enough.

But then along came Sadie. I loved her from the moment she ripped her head out of the halter when I turned her out after breakfast. She sprinted to the far pasture as fast as her long legs could carry her, a streak of dark chocolate, running for the first ten minutes of turnout before settling at the round bale.

She became mine in my head long before my husband adopted her a year later as a Christmas present to me. Because the barn was an hour away, I saw her only once a week for a few months before I brought her much closer to home—a small, family-run barn just a mile from my house. It was a partial self-care situation, with a dusty indoor barn circled by stalls; small, dry turnouts; a large ring; and a smaller round pen. The plan was for me to muck her stall and provide dinner each day. The barn would feed her in the mornings and turn her out with hay.

When moving day finally arrived, there was a flurry of activity as she met her pasture mates and settled into her small stall. I tidied up her tack trunk and prepared her food for the morning. I watched her for a while, made sure her stall was pristine and her water full.

I was 34, and I had just brought home my first horse.

I had dreamed in ponies and horses my entire life but never had more than a handful of trail rides and one disastrous week of summer camp. And now I had my beautiful Sadie Mae.

The tricky part: how was I going to connect with my sweet mare? I didn't want a horse with dead eyes that went through the motions like the trail horses I had last ridden, but I wanted her to see me as the leader. She was trained as a racer with a second career as a dressage school horse with buttons I had no idea how to push. She had no bond with me beyond the fact that I was a regular in her life who often showed up with food — big motivation for our equine friends, certainly, but I knew there could be something deeper to this relationship.

Chris Irwin, a world-renowned trainer who did not grow up with horses either, uses a deep understanding of herd dynamics and horse body language to help him connect with the horses he trains. His goal is to develop a bond that is reciprocal, with horse and rider actively seeking out each other's company:

> *"When a horse consistently experiences that you make it feel better than it does on its own – then it focuses on you more and more, and WANTS to be with you. It needs to be that simple – does your horse feel better with you than it does on its own or when it is with other horses?"*

This view of training looks at the connection between horse and rider as primary to the relationship. It's about benevolent leadership — a far cry from some training practices that would see horses "trained" into submission without consideration of their needs (like so many rental trail horses).

And because professional horse trainers are a luxury not everyone can afford, many choose to learn how to train on their own. Some horse owners sample from a variety of training philosophies and practices, while others buy into an entire program that may not center the horse and its needs.

Sadie and I started on our path to connection by getting to know each other with daily interaction. I read and watched other trainers, going to clinics and asking an annoying number of questions for a person who could only afford to audit.

It took me years of practice and patience with myself to learn, and the road was often frustrating. I didn't always know what I didn't know, and sometimes I had a sense that even the professional trainers I admired were looking for more connection than they had achieved with their horses.

It wasn't just me trying to figure out the best way to build a relationship. Entire schools of trainers were evolving and constantly refining the ways in which they learned how to connect with their horses and transmit that learning to horse owners. Buck Brannaman has spoken candidly about his early days riding when it was more about muscling a horse into shape than helping them succeed. In his own words: "We would run a colt in, suck him down in the halter, tie up a hind leg and slap a saddle on him whether he liked it or not."

Attending a Ray Hunt clinic changed Brannaman's entire training philosophy from aggressive training and "...riding colts...with broken fingernails and claw marks and doing the best [he] could," to a style that asks, "'What will my horse get out of this if I get what I want?'"

Developing a horse in this way means creating a connection that acknowledges them as a partner, not simply a beast to be conquered.

My lovely mare taught me what it means to bond with a horse. Sadie was patient and kind. Over the years of trial and error, I learned about:

- Reading body language
- Letting horses be horses
- How to approach training
- The idea of feel
- What respect actually means

Sadie, and the horses that came after her, taught me there is more to owning horses than riding, and keeping the horse's needs in mind is what deepens your bond with them.

This book will help you build respect and willingness with your equine friend without force or coercion. It starts with understanding what connection is and why it's important before moving through groundwork, riding exercises, and ways to improve yourself for your horse. Each chapter provides a selection of exercises and activities either directly related to handling and riding or designed to support your horse in ways that improve their mind and body.

For people who have owned horses for years, some of this work might seem elementary, while other exercises might be just the thing to continue on your path. Use this book to explore more ways to connect with your horse and to discover areas that pique your horse's interest and seem ripe for more exploration. You might find your dressage horse loves to work a trail obstacle course. Your steady trail horse might love working equitation or speeding around a jump course. You both might relax into the pleasures of overnight trail rides with friends.

And for those new to horses, staring at your equine companion and wondering where to begin? This book provides a roadmap to help you explore your relationship so you can take the time you need to become true partners. Each exercise helps you cultivate confidence and connection to your horse with the goal of developing an alliance that can take you in any direction you choose with a willing, enthusiastic partner.

After years together, Sadie and I developed a special bond. She was the patient, affectionate, and intelligent first horse everyone deserves. Even though our learning curve to connection was steep, the climb was worth the view from the top. I learned and respected her desire to retire from riding to focus on in-hand and liberty work, and she rewarded me with an obvious pleasure in my company and a clear desire for our time together.

At the root of all the work is the idea that horses and humans at every level of experience can learn to savor each other's company, to enjoy whatever tasks are ahead, and to go as willing partners—together.

PART I

GROUNDWORK

"Trust and respect are two-way streets. We want the horse to accept us as leaders of the herd, to guide them safely, and to provide protection and comfort. In return, they will give us their respect, and willing submission to our ideas about what to do next, and when and where. But this respect can only be based on well-deserved trust."
Walter Zettl

The halter was empty of my horse's head before I even realized she was gone. With her sharp tug up and back, I was left holding a dangling lead rope and staring at the dusty hind end of hooves flinging dirt clods as she sprinted across the pasture.

Tearing her head out of the halter was not the only issue regarding Sadie's behavior. She was never mean or malicious, but she was accustomed to moving in whatever direction she felt like when she had the idea. I had never seen her under saddle, but I had wrestled with her down the barn aisle and into her stall for weeks before finally watching a groundwork clinic put on by the rescue where I was volunteering. This clinic taught a series of simple movements, done while on the ground, to engage a horse's mind while moving their feet.

It was only when I stepped into the role of the leader with these simple, consistent activities that Sadie could finally relax. She was telling me where to go and when because someone had to do it — in my inexperience, she recognized that I was not up to the task.

But after the clinic I stepped up. Regular groundwork sessions brought Sadie peace of mind. She stopped setting the pace as we walked; she moved her body out of the way; she waited for me to release her from her halter and walked calmly away a few paces before her instinct toward joyful galloping took hold.

Groundwork is a way to set the tone for every activity you do with your horse. It makes them a safer equine companion because they look to you for guidance instead of taking matters into their own hands (hooves).

Groundwork is appropriate for:

- Old horses
- Young horses
- Big horses
- Mini ponies
- Horses in work
- Horses on layup
- Horses at rest
- Retired horses

In short, every horse (and horse owner) benefits from groundwork. And make no mistake about it: every time you interact with your horse you are training them. So why not use those interactions to build a better bond?

CHAPTER 1

DESENSITIZING

"You can watch wild horses for a whole day and nothing astounding may happen. They graze, they drink, they seem to meander without obvious direction. It is all subtlety.... When we do it right, there won't be much drama. You learn to increase your attention and you train your mind to let more information [come] to you....You learn to have more patience, you learn to watch, and you learn to let it come to you. To train horses well you have to learn to observe subtleties." Paul Belasik

Horses are scared of two things: things that move and things that don't move. Your relationship with a well-mannered horse begins with desensitizing. Desensitizing makes a scary, horse-eating object not frightening (or at least tolerable).

The idea is to introduce a new object slowly, encouraging them to explore it and building their confidence and trust in you.

You aren't trying to create a "dead" or dull horse. You do want a horse that is curious and lively. Desensitizing doesn't dampen a horse's personality. It makes your horse safer and more predictable. You won't worry about a plastic bag blowing past or a car starting sending your horse running for the hills.

Desensitizing follows the fundamental training principle of approach and retreat. It's a simple process.

- Identify the scary thing.
- Show it to your horse at a distance.
- Gradually decrease the distance between the object and your horse.
- Encourage your horse to step toward the object.

It is important to remember to start slowly, build gradually, and reward your horse with a break every time they try to give you what you ask for.

A word about treats

Treats can be a useful motivational tool, especially in the early days of training. But keep in mind that treats can also create a fat horse who mugs you every time you step into the pasture. The solution?

- Treat, but include verbal praise with the treat.
- When the horse learns a behavior, replace the treat with verbal praise.
- Only gives treats when the horse's head is straight forward (unless you're using a treat to help them stretch).

If you are opposed to treats entirely or your horse has dietary concerns, rest assured that you can still get good results with consistency and rest as a reward.

It all starts with you

Before you can begin to desensitize to objects, it is crucial to desensitize your horse to YOU.

You must be able to touch anywhere on your horse's body. This contact is essential for not only things like treating an injury but also in everyday work. If your horse kicks out when you touch their legs, they are unsafe. This process also helps you to bond with your horse.

Before picking any objects to start desensitizing, follow the next three steps until your horse is relaxed and willing to have your hands anywhere on their body.

Step one

Your horse needs to accept firm — not harsh — contact all over their body from nose to tail and ears to hooves. You cannot begin any other desensitizing until your horse accepts contact with your hands.

Start at the shoulder and the side of the neck, moving your hands in long strokes down their shoulders and flanks. Use firm contact so it isn't annoying to them.

If your horse is unsure about your hands on their body, go even more slowly.

- Have them face you.
- Hold out a hand.
- Lean away.
- Wait for them to investigate your hand
- Drop your hand when you feel their muzzle and treat them with rest.

Gradually you will proceed to more sensitive areas: the face, the back, and the legs. If they flinch in a particular area, pause in that place until they settle, then back off.

Step two

Another important desensitizing action is getting your horse to lower their head when you ask.

A horse should lower their head when asked to do so with slight pressure at the top of their head. Ask your horse to lower their head every time you halter. Do not fall into the easy trap of haltering from the front or standing on tiptoe. You should be able to drape your arm over their neck to easily slide the halter over their nose.

- Place a hand on their poll (the top of the head between the ears).
- Let the weight of your hand be pressure enough, or add a slight push downward.
- Wait until they drop their head away from your hand.

When they drop their head, even slightly, release the pressure and take a break. They will respond more quickly with practice. Their poll should be at shoulder level when you ask – no higher, no lower.

Troubleshooting

If they back in response to the request to lower their head, follow them and keep asking.

If they raise their head or turn away, do your best to follow them with your hand. For very tall horses, adding slight downward pressure from a halter can help.

Do not skip this step, and spend time on it especially if your horse is tall. Horses not trained to do this soon learn that they can throw their heads up to avoid bridling, haltering, and requests for movement under saddle.

Step three

The final desensitizing mission is in the mouth.

Rub your horse's gums, peel back their lips, stroke their muzzle. A horse's nose is extremely sensitive, so respect that as you work.

This may seem awkward, but a horse needs to accept hands on their muzzle and in their mouth for bitting and health and dental work.

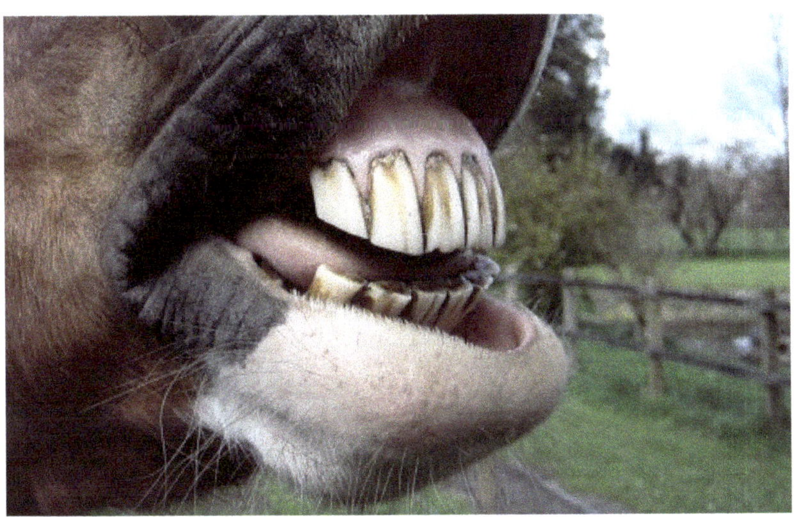

Do not skip this step because of teeth, but be cautious, especially if you have a horse prone to "mouthiness" (or teething, as with young horses).

For an easier time bridling, combine lowering the head with this step.

- Ask your horse to lower their head.
- Insert a thumb in the corner of their mouth where the bit sits.
- When they open their mouth, remove your thumb and praise them.

Horses introduced to this gentle way of bridling are less stressed about taking a bit. They trust you won't bang it on their teeth or shove it harshly in their mouth.

Desensitizing to objects

Once you can handle your horse everywhere, lower their head, and touch all over their face, it's time to start working with objects.

Of course, you won't be able to predict every potentially scary thing the world throws at your horse. So why bother trying?

- Desensitizing builds confidence and curiosity in your horse.
- Desensitizing exposes horses to some everyday objects that might cause fear.
- Desensitizing builds trust in you as the herd leader — if you aren't scared, why should they be?

Regardless of the object, the basic process is the same.

- Introduce the object while on the ground and at a distance.
- Start quietly, then make noise with the object if it makes noise.
- Allow your horse to move around if they need to.
- Follow their movement without increasing your energy (or the object's).
- When your horse's feet stop moving and they relax (lower their head, lick their lips, or make chewing motions with their mouth), instantly stop and praise.
- Start the noise again after a break with lots of praise.
- Stop when they relax.

Repeat this process on both sides of the horse, gradually moving closer (to or with the object).

It's just that simple. Eventually, you'll desensitize while mounted, but always start on the ground.

The Big List

As prey animals, horses are poised to flee. Because the world is a scary place, it's impossible to desensitize to every object. You can't predict the strange things a horse will leap away from.

When you expose your horse to common items around the house and barn, they gain confidence. Then if they do spook, they are less likely to take off and more apt to "spook in place" (infinitely more desirable). Here's a list to get you started.

1. Ropes and training equipment

Your horse needs to be okay with all of your training equipment. This includes:

- Ropes (see sidebar)
- Stick/string
- Whips
- Stick/flag

They should be responsive to the equipment when you ask but relaxed in its neutral presence.

2. Clippers

Start with clippers:

- Turned off
- Turned on at a distance
- Turned on at the shoulder
- Down the neck
- Down the back
- Down the legs
- To the muzzle
- To the ears

3. Umbrellas

Use them in all ways: open, closed, flapping, twirling, above them, beside them, etc.

4. Tarps

Tarps can simulate water crossings (which scare some horses). They can also be draped over and dragged behind your horse or worn as a cape by a rider. Start small so it is easy for you to manage, and, as always, go slow.

5. Bicycles

Enlist the help of a bicycle-riding friend to ride circles around you and your horse. Start by letting your horse sniff and inspect a bicycle at rest, then walk slowly by it without a rider. Next, have your friend slowly ride the bike past, increasing speed and movement as your horse is comfortable.

6. Branches

Walk your horse by fallen branches, swing a branch with rustling leaves as you walk, rub the branch on your horse's back. Walk your horse over fallen limbs. Snap twigs, rustle dead leaves.

A note about ropes

Many people treat ropes as a casual desensitizing item, but they are so much more than that. A horse desensitized to ropes around its legs is less likely to injure themselves if their legs are caught in a rope (or a wire). Ropes are also used in various training settings, so take more time with this until they can tolerate all kinds of ropes on their body and legs, even when they are in motion.

- *Use a long lead rope. Stand diagonally away from your horse's shoulder with the hand closest to them held at your shoulder level (like a stop sign almost). This keeps them from getting any ideas about moving toward you.*
- *Swing the rope around all four feet, one at a time., starting at the front.*
- *Rhythmically swing the rope up and over their back, letting it slide down their barrel.*
- *If the rope slips and doesn't quite get over their back, that's okay. The rhythm is the most important thing. A steady rhythm becomes predictable for them and helps them relax.*
- *Keep swinging the rope over until their feet stay steady or they drop their head and lick or chew.*
- *Fling the rope down their back and then around their legs and hindquarters.*
- *When your horse is comfortable with ropes standing still, try the same action as they move.*
- *You cannot repeat this exercise too many times.*

---

7. Little kids

Little kids present many opportunities for desensitizing practice. Your horse must be safe for kids who don't know how to behave around horses. This is especially true if you will be at shows or on trails with people unused to horses.

To desensitize a horse to little kids, ask friends to run around and make sudden noises on all sides of your horse. Tell them to pop out from behind a building and scream. You are not trying to upset your horse, but you want to get them used to small, unexpected events.

8. Trucks

Some horses get upset by the sight of trucks and other large machinery. Walk your horse by trucks, and then have the trucks drive by the pasture and honk. As a last stage, have the trucks come behind you on the road (slowly and carefully on a quiet road). The same procedures can be followed for tractors, combines, lawnmowers, dirt bikes, and ATVs.

9. Flags

This activity is invaluable if you plan on doing drill team maneuvers, but tying flags all over your horse is an excellent activity to help keep them calm when pieces of paper or fabric blow by. You can tie flags off the halter, saddle, legs, tail, etc.

You can also desensitize to flags or fluttering fabric by tying long bits of material to a training stick and running it all over your horse's face, legs, and body.

10. Balloons

In the same way you used the flags, grab some inflated balloons and attach them to a long string. You can bounce them near your horse or slide them across their neck and back. Eventually, you will be able to tie a balloon to your horse's tail or saddle while they stand quietly. If you are "lucky," one might pop and offer more desensitizing opportunities.

11. Water

To desensitize reluctant bathers, start slowly. Some horses are scared of the hose, some of the water, and some are terrified by both.

Show your horse the hose, turn on the water, and begin by spraying water on their hooves. Move slowly up each front leg, stopping and holding it anywhere they start to dance around or get nervous. When they settle, stop spraying (retreat) and rest before resuming. Continue to spray on the rear hooves, moving slowly up those legs, too.

Come back to the front legs and move to the shoulder, then the withers, then over the back and down the hindquarters. Most horses do not like water in their face, so try to keep the spray over their face gentle and brief. Be careful not to get water in their ears.

End by offering your horse a drink from the hose. Many horses like to play with the water once they get used to it.

12. Bridges

Horses like solid ground under their feet, so bridges represent a giant leap of faith in their people.

To desensitize to a bridge, the best thing to do is lead your horse past the bridge first, going slowly, letting the bridge become familiar. When you approach the bridge to walk on it, think confident, bridge-crossing thoughts. This confidence reaches your horse through the lead rope.

If your horse is nervous, ask for one hoof on the bridge, then turn around and walk away. Repeat. Ask for two hooves, then walk away. Repeat. Rest at the bridge.

Gradually ask your horse to stand their whole body on the bridge, then walk off. Eventually, your horse will understand that the bridge will not collapse and that walking on it is no big deal.

You can also set up boards on the ground as part of an obstacle course, graduating to bridges as your horse's confidence builds.

13. Squeaky toys

Squeak that toy all over your horse's body, following the same rhythm and progression that you used for the plastic bag.

14. Floppy hats/baseball caps

Some horses lose their minds at the sight of a baseball cap or a hat. Don't let yours be one of them. Wear the cap, but rub it over the horse also.

15. Strollers

Borrow a friend's baby stroller, and run it by your horse. Roll it on your horse. Roll it under your horse.

A common-sense caution: You should not have a baby in the stroller. Feel free to substitute a baby doll if you are going for authenticity.

16. Ladders

Big and small, step stools and extension ladders: Walk your horse around them, and have people walk by your horse carrying them.

Clang them open, slam them shut, and lean them on your horse at the end of the day (gently!). Climb up one right next to your horse.

17. Pitchforks/rakes

Some horses fear everyday farm implements, but you can desensitize them so thoroughly that they beg for a back scratch with the rake.

18. Car horns

If you plan to ride on or near a road, your horse must be desensitized to car horns.

Many well-intentioned drivers signal their presence with a beep, which may upset your horse. Have a friend beep short beeps in a rhythm as you move your horse closer to the car. When you think your horse is calm and accepting, have your friend beep unexpectedly. Make sure and send your neighbors a nice card or some flowers when you are done with this exercise.

19. Pulling objects

Your horse is designed to flee from things that chase, so pulling an object can be challenging.

You might start by placing the object on their sides (perhaps tied to the saddle or stirrups), gradually letting it drop to drag behind them. Give them space to adjust to the object, and start this at the walk.

20. Rain ponchos and slickers

You may, at some point, need to wear rain gear to care for your horse (or to put it on while you're in the saddle). The last thing you want is a panicked horse running across a muddy pasture in the pouring rain. Plan for this by exposing your horse to you in a raincoat well before the rain falls.

Try a bright yellow slicker or a fluttery poncho - whatever you might throw on in a storm.

Slicker Break A Bronco

When you're breakin' out a bronc,
better get them slicker broke.
For you'll have to try it sometime
when it isn't any joke.

When the wind begins a blowin'
till it snaps their mane and tail,
And a big black cloud's a comin'
full o' lightnin', rain and hail.

You know if you get off them
he will likely pull away,
So you try it in the saddle
and you're hopin' that you stay.

But your horse starts a buckin'
When you get it halfway on.
While your arms and sleeves are tangled,
then he throws you and he's gone.

Your slicker's torn and busted,
and the wind has took your hat,
And you see your horse and saddle
go a-driftin' down the flat.

Bout that time you get an idea
and you don't forget it, pal:
Better slicker-break a bronco
in a mighty good corral
-Bruce Kiskaddon-

CHAPTER 2

THE SIX BASIC MOVEMENTS

"It's not so much what we do, it's how we do what we do. And all you are trying to do is get this horse to where you can operate the life in his body, through his legs to his feet, through his mind. The mind might come last because he don't understand. But you have to give him space to learn." Ray Hunt

Groundwork in the Six Basic Movements is the cornerstone of your relationship with your horse. Controlling the body on the ground builds respect and translates directly into riding.

- It's a safe place to establish boundaries and get to know how your horse reacts.
- It's the place where you make an offer to your horse at the speed your horse is comfortable with.
- It's also the place where you begin to develop curiosity in your horse.
- It's going slowly and smoothly with as little pressure as needed (but enough to get the job done).

Groundwork is where you:

1. Learn to communicate in a language you both understand
2. Establish yourself as the firm but fair leader of your herd
3. Develop a bond of trust and affection

If you cannot make something happen on the ground, it will be infinitely more challenging in the saddle.

Your goal in all groundwork training sessions should be clear communication to get a response at the lightest request possible.

A couple of tips

- Start as slowly as you need to.
- Set attainable goals for each training session.
- Reward the try (if they attempt to do what you ask, reward them).
- Consider every session on the ground as training.
- Stop on success.

That last one is important. If you find yourself getting impatient or frustrated, chances are good that your horse is feeling the same thing. Back off, start from the last positive step, and end there.

Know that horses can progress in leaps and bounds one day and then seemingly relapse to "bad" behavior, only to surge forward the next day. The younger your horse, the more inconsistent their responses will be at first. This is normal.

Be patient, be consistent, and reward the slightest attempt from your horse to fulfill your requests.

Equipment

You do not need special, pricey equipment for training. A rope halter with two knots on the nose works well (you can even make your own). This type of halter does not allow a horse to resist by leaning into the nose like a web halter might. A 12-foot lead rope is a good length to start with.

If all you have is a web halter and a ten-foot lead rope, start with that. Remember that a horse is reading your body language more than any equipment you have, and body language is free.

Other tools extend your reach to keep your horse at a safe distance. They are also very helpful in reinforcing cues you give your horse on the ground. Remember to desensitize your horse to your chosen tools before using them (see Chapter 1).

You can use a stick with a flag on the end, a lunge or dressage whip, or a fiberglass stick-and-string

Safety Note

The following are brief descriptions of sometimes complicated actions. There are problems a novice should never try to address alone (i.e., rearing and bucking).

For all others:

- Proceed with safety and caution.
- Ask for help when you need it.
- Recognize your limitations.
- Do not undertake a maneuver that makes you nervous or anxious, as this anxiety is transmitted to your horse.

Remember that this is a process. Take the time to enjoy your work together. You are laying the foundation for a beautiful partnership.

The Six Basic Movements

Movement 1: Lowering the head

A horse should lower their head at the lightest request. Not only is this useful for safe haltering, but a lowered head is an immediate stress reliever for horses. It's a good practice when your horse gets distracted or begins to bring their energy up.

Additionally, lowering the head teaches a horse to release from pressure on their poll and behind their ears. This makes training a horse to tie and lead much easier.

There are two ways to accomplish this.

Option A: With a halter

- Stand either facing the direction your horse is facing or slightly in front of them and to the side (make sure they can see you from one eye).
- Hold the knot of the halter and apply downward pressure.
- Do not try to pull their head down. Just add pressure so they feel the halter make contact.
- Stop applying pressure when they drop their head, release, then ask again until they drop their head.

- If they immediately throw their head up when you release, follow the movement of their head. Keep asking until they drop it even the tiniest fraction.

Taking care of your horse's feelings

Best case scenario, our horses are curious, engaged, and willing partners. But too often in our quest to move the feet and become the leader we forget to check in with how our horse is feeling

Consider the dulled lesson horse. They are checked out as a protective measure against beginners who accidentally pull their heads and kick their sides. They eventually comply. And though many of them would be considered "lazy" or "stubborn," this slow responsive is protective and helps them do their job.

We don't want this dullness for our horses. We start with groundwork to establish ourselves as worthy of our horse's partnership, which means paying close attention to how they respond to what we're asking.

Evoke positive emotions by backing off before anxiety becomes overwhelming and give them time to try to find the answer to your question. If your horse is nervous, dull, or unsure, start by asking "yes" questions. These are the questions your horse already knows the answer to and can help build their confidence in themselves — and you.

And never underestimate the power of a bond with you that's created by providing ample food, friends, and forage. Caring for their body can help them find the physical balance they need to become more emotionally adept and responsive.

Option B: With a hand on the poll

- Stand facing the same direction your horse is facing.
- Place your hand on their poll — the slight rise between and slightly behind the ears — and wait for them to lower it away from your hand.
- If they lift their head higher or move around to evade, stay until they drop it.

Movement 2: Backing

Backing your horse is what it sounds like – backing your horse out of your personal space or away from the area they are in. The goal is a willing, energetic, prompt back up when asked.

Why?

- To move them from your space (safety)
- To unlock their feet
- To engage their brain

Your horse needs to understand that your space is yours — they are an invited guest. Think of it this way: You can walk into their house and rearrange all their furniture, but they must wait to be invited into your driveway. There are three ways to teach the back up.

Option A: Halter pressure

- Stand just in front of their shoulder facing their hind legs.
- Holding the knot under their chin, add backward pressure on their halter and say, "Back."
- If they are new to this, release pressure when they shift their weight back.
- Gradually ask for one step, then two, etc.

Option B: Hand on nose or chest

For smaller movement and to get your horse in sync with your steps, back by applying slight pressure to their nose across the place just below where the halter rests or to the center of their chest.

In the beginning, ask for a single step at a time, letting their movement backward naturally release the pressure of your hand.

If they evade the touch on the nose, follow them with your hand and do not release until they move back. Do not increase the pressure. Be patient.

Option C: Energy

If you need to keep space between you and your horse for safety reasons, use the energy of the halter and lead rope to teach them to back.

- Stand in front of your horse, facing them (slightly to the left or right).
- Lean your body weight forward, lift your hand, and say, "Back."
- As with halter pressure, reward a shift in weight or one single step by releasing.
- If the horse does not move, add "pressure" by lifting the lead rope up and snapping it down until they move. Don't be dainty or just annoying about it. Make yourself clear once so you don't have to nag multiple times.
- Immediately release.

If you opt for this method, take care to use a rope halter without metal hardware. Whacking your horse in the chin with an extra-large bull snap is inconsiderate and unnecessary. A rope knot transmits the same message more compassionately.

You may need to snap the rope several times, but don't stop until they move even the smallest step back. Do not move your own feet — make them move away from you. The key is, as Buck Brannaman says, "Gentle in what you do; firm in how you do it."

Movement 3: Moving forward

Moving forward is another way to teach your horse to release from the pressure of the halter. It's helpful for everything from tying to bridling.

- If you have worked on getting your horse to lower their head, they are primed for this movement.
- Stand next to your haltered horse, facing forward.

- Hold the leadrope in both hands low across your waist.
- Step forward, taking the slack out of the rope.
- Your horse should follow, adding slack but not crowding you.

Troubleshooting

- Do not look back. Look in the direction you want to go.
- If their feet are sticky, walk to the left or the right. Stop when they take a step. Then move again.
- Do not increase pressure, but change direction if you are not getting any movement.

"Drawing" your horse

Another option is to motion your horse forward toward you. This forward movement type is also called "drawing" your horse in liberty work (see Chapter 4).

- Back your horse away from you and face them.
- Lay the lead rope over your palms, and apply slight pressure towards you (not pulling, just making them aware).
- Lean back slightly to invite them towards you.
- Release as they step forward.
- When you want them to stop, lean slightly toward them (the same energy you used to back them).
- Pause and reward.

Movement 4: Lateral flexion

Lateral flexion refers to bending your horse's neck to either side. This type of flexibility is necessary to increase the quality and ease of a horse's movement. A horse that is supple and light in the body is more sensitive to cues, requires only a light touch, and has responsive steering under saddle.

To work towards this:

- Stand next to your haltered horse at about the place where you would sit in the saddle.
- From their near side, have the leadrope in your left hand with the excess rope draped over their back.
- Drape your right arm over their back. Stand there for a moment if this is an unfamiliar action for them.

- Apply pressure to the lead rope, moving it towards where the horn or pommel of the saddle is.
- You are looking for a slight response: ear flicked to you or the eye turning to you.
- Release immediately and let them straighten their neck.
- Repeat, releasing pressure as soon as they change their focus to you.

The critical thing to remember is to release the pressure the moment your horse does what you ask. Warwick Schiller once demonstrated teaching a horse to flex laterally with such light pressure that it did not snap the piece of horse hair he had attached his lead rope to his halter with.

This is your goal. Repeat on both sides until your horse becomes lighter and gives more with less pressure. Eventually, you will feel them start to reach for you and you reach for them. This is the start of developing feel.

Clicker training

Clicker training can be incorporated into any of the training ideas here. Clickers are hand-held noisemakers often used in dog training. The idea is that when a horse does what you ask, you click and offer a treat.

Eventually, the horse recognizes the click as the reward and responds to the commands without a carrot or a cookie. Some trainers use clickers to get their horses to touch an object. This can lead to more complex tricks, such as playing fetch or following the tip of a whip at liberty.

Movement 5: Release hindquarters

Releasing the hindquarters is also referred to as turning on the forehand. You ask your horse to move their hips to one side or the other while their body is bent, crossing the inside hind foot in front of the outside hind.

This exercise increases a horse's suppleness, builds strength and balance, and creates better control of the horse's "engine" (their hind end)

You'll want to establish good lateral flexion before you ask the hindquarters to swing away.

- Stand two or three feet away from your horse's shoulder and raise the hand nearest to their face to block any movement of the head towards you.

- In the other hand, you should have enough leadrope to swing in a circle, but not an excessive amount you cannot handle.
- If you choose to use a stick and flag or stick and string, hold it in the hand with the excess rope like a tennis racquet.
- Ask your horse to flex towards you as you walk towards the back hip.
- The back foot closest to you should cross in front of the back foot farthest away as the hip swings over.
- If this is brand new for your horse, reward any correct movement by releasing pressure (stop asking). Repeat on both sides.

- If your horse is an old hand at this, gradually ask for more steps across. You can also work towards a lighter request — your horse may eventually be able to release with just a glance at their hip.

Troubleshooting

- If they step towards you in the front, block the movement with your hand.

- Get flexion before asking for the hip to move.
- If the hip does not budge, add a tap with the stick, flag, or swinging lead rope.
- If the foot closest to you does not cross over, keep asking until it does, then immediately release and praise.
- The most skillful horse people work towards getting in time with the feet — ask for a horse to move over when the inside foot is leaving the ground, and step towards the horse as they step over.

Movement 6: Release shoulders

Releasing the shoulders helps with steering and lightness in the front end. Releasing the shoulders starts with lateral flexion at about 45 degrees (it's closer to 90 when you release the hind).

Your body position is critical here. Imagine a laser beam in your belly button and a bubble around you. You are moving toward your horse and asking them not only to move in the direction your laser beam is pointing but also to stay out of your bubble. You want your horse to step back and away, and you'll time your request to step away to match the moment the front foot farthest away from you leaves the ground.

- Stand facing their neck (either side, but let's assume the near side).
- Hold the leadrope in your right hand, about two feet of it, at the approximate angle of your reins if you were riding.
- Apply pressure backwards with the right hand to begin the movement.
- Once you have a solid back up, stop moving your feet back and move them towards the horse.
- You are looking for the left foot to step back or away and the right foot to step over.
- Once you have that, stop and praise.

- You can increase the pressure by tapping your horse on the cheek with your left hand and just behind the halter with your right in a one-two beat.
- Keep the pressure steady until something changes.
- Repeat until you get a lighter response with less pressure.

Troubleshooting

- If your horse steps towards you, increase the pressure with a flag or other training aid until they move out of your space.
- If they step forward, angle your body slightly toward them to drive them first back and then over.
- If your horse is tall and can avoid your hands, use your training aid to reinforce your cue.

CHAPTER 3

COMBINING DESENSITIZING AND THE SIX BASIC MOVEMENTS

"If you are only a student of technique, then the options become very limited. On the other hand, when you are a student of the horse, the options are unlimited." Mark Rashid

The exercises that combine desensitizing with the Six Basic Movements serve two functions.

1. You are helping your horse understand that you will take care of them as the leader of the herd.
2. You are introducing a variety of scenarios they might encounter and encouraging curiosity.

As you progress through these exercises, mixing up training with targeted activities to engage their mind, move their body, and get to the feet (not necessarily in that order) can be helpful.

All of these are excellent preparation that translate directly to riding exercises. They are a great way to build confidence in yourself, lightness in your horse, and softness in their mind.

Leading

Leading your horse seems simple — you put on the halter, and off you go, right?

You may struggle to get their feet moving if you have not taught your horse to give to pressure at the poll (by lowering their head).

Practice proper leading, and you'll have a safer horse on the ground who follows you at whatever speed and direction you set.

- Start on your horse's near side.
- Back them out of your space if needed. The optimal position is with their head at least a foot away from your leading hand. This allows you to turn without running into your horse.
- Hold your lead rope loosely across the front of your hips and step forward.
- They should willingly step forward when the slack comes out of the rope and applies pressure to their poll.
- Practice speeding up, slowing down, and changing directions. Eventually, they will pay attention to your feet and keep the slack out of the rope on their own.

Troubleshooting

- Do not increase the pressure if their feet get sticky and won't move. Walk to the side until they move, stop and praise, then start again.
- If they run into you and don't respect your space while you are leading, back them up. They are responsible for maintaining the space between you and the slack in the rope.
- Use a stick and flag and start this exercise with your horse against a fence. The flag should be in the hand farthest from the horse. If they don't step forward in a timely fashion, slip that stick and flag behind you to tap their shoulder.

Tying

The best way to teach your horse to tie is to tie them — often and for varying periods. Make sure they are good at yielding to pressure on the poll, and use a blocker tie for safety.

A "patience pole" is used in some circles. This is a post set in concrete. The idea is to tie your horse and let them thrash it out until they give up, exhausted.

Trouble is, horses can seriously injure themselves on this setup, and you are creating a defeated horse, not a willing one. Yes, your horse needs to be able to tie and stand quietly for many reasons. No, they don't have to be frantic and desperate to flee to achieve this. Make it pleasant for them to learn how to tie instead of stressful.

- Start with short periods.
- Give them room to move their bodies so they feel less trapped.
- Make sure they understand releasing to poll pressure first.
- Gradually increase the time you ask them to stand.
- Move on to crossties when the blocker tie is rock solid.

Back in a circle

Backing your horse in a circle is a delicate maneuver that requires you to be able to release their hindquarters with a look.

Essentially you are guiding the hind end as you back them, moving the point of the hip with a look or a tap. Too firm a look or tap and they swing completely away; too light, and they continue to back straight. This activity increases their lightness to your cues and suppleness in their body. It makes them a more responsive, agile horse under saddle.

It also gets them thinking about you as they move their feet while keeping the focus on your connection.

- Start by asking your horse to follow your movement with their nose as you walk around them. You want to to remain steady in one place while you do this, turning but not moving forward or backward.
- Once your horse is following you with their nose (but without moving their feet), begin to ask them to back.
- These two motions combined will send them backward in a circle.
- Repeat in both directions.

Troubleshooting

- If they back straight, bump the lead rope slightly to make sure they are sticking with you as you move around them.
- If they seem stiff, move slowly and work on suppleness with more lateral flexion.
- Back circles in both directions. This is usually easier on one side, so be ready to adjust what (and how) you're asking.
- Make sure they are following you with their nose before you ask them to back.

Backing through and over obstacles

Backing your horse through obstacles helps to build trust. Remember, they cannot see directly behind themselves, which requires an enormous amount of faith in you.

Get them confident in backing a circle in both directions before you start.

Start backing through obstacles by backing your horse into their stall at night if they are stalled. Give them a "step up" verbal command if they have a stall door to step over. This is helpful for backing over poles and onto bridges.

From there, it is a simple matter to arrange a tunnel of cones and move your horse through them, first forward, then backward, using your body language and a reminder tap from the flag or lunge whip if necessary.

If they are soft and responsive to the backup command and release their front and hind end, it's just a matter of going slowly through or over whatever course you set up.

Send in both directions

As you gain your horse's trust and get them more willing to move their feet, it's time to teach and practice lunging movements. Sending a horse in both directions is about controlling the horse's direction and speed. This is also helpful with trailer loading and moving a horse through gates.

Additionally, this continues to reinforce the idea that you are the leader of your two-horse herd, telling your horse:

- When to move their feet
- Where to go
- How quickly to get there

This is all about body language, so it would be best to have an experienced person with you when you start this to evaluate the placement of your body. You must angle your body so your horse knows you are sending them forward and in a specific direction.

You are pushing your horse forward from just behind their shoulder (the driveline). Your body guides the movement, with your belly button pointing towards the back of the shoulder to move them forward.

Alternate sides of your horse when you work on this to ensure each side gets equal time (and you don't build a "one-sided" horse).

- Stand in the round pen with your haltered horse (or in a small field with no other horses if you do not have a round pen).
- Back them away from you, staying where you are but asking them to move out.
- If you want your horse to start clockwise, hold the lead rope up in your right hand (and a lunge whip. stick and string combo, or stick and flag in your left).
- Extend your right hand, pointing in the direction you want your horse to go.
- Step towards their shoulder/drive line.
- You are looking for a horse to step away first and then circle with an even bend

the entire length of their body from nose to tail.

- If your horse does not respond forward after stepping away, escalate pressure by wiggling the flag or stick/string/lunge whip at their hip and back legs.
- If they don't step their shoulder over first, use the flag or the rope on their shoulder.
- To stop, lower the leading hand and drop your energy. You can add some pressure to their inside hip, asking them to swing it away and face you.

Troubleshooting

- Start small, and don't whack them if they don't respond immediately, especially if this is new for them (or you). You don't want to train your horse to leap forward when you ask for a walk.
- If you do not want to use a whip, you can use a longer lead rope and swing the end to get them moving if they hesitate to move off.
- Keep your eyes focused on the shoulder, not your horse's eye. For some horses, eye contact is too threatening and makes them nervous. By dropping your eyes

to your horse's shoulder or focusing on the direction you want them to go, you are sending a clear signal and keeping the "door" in front of them open.

- If the shoulder starts to fall in, brush the flag against it to encourage your horse to maintain their bend.
- If they keep looking to the outside of the circle, bump the lead rope to get them to tip their nose inside.
- For more desensitizing, wave the flag or stick and string away from their body in a rhythmic motion. Eventually, bring it closer and place it on their body. The goal is to respect the tool when you use it to ask them to move but to be unfazed when it's neutral.
- Keep your leading hand neutral when your horse does what you ask. Only bring the energy and the hand up when they stop or when you want to change gaits.
- If your horse refuses to move forward, check your body position first. You may be too far ahead and unwittingly telling them to stop. You may also have them too far away from you. Try shortening the length of the lead rope a bit for more control.
- You can work at all gaits this way, but be mindful not to lunge your horse in circles endlessly. This does not help engage the mind at all.

"Squeeze" between a fence

Once they understand what you are asking when you send them in both directions, you can vary this exercise by forming a chute with cones and a fence. Send your horse between these cones, then turn them by releasing the inside hip to go in the other direction.

Send into a trailer

You, too, can have a horse that loads itself into a trailer. This is the culminating event to sending: looping the lead rope over your horse's neck and simply pointing to the open trailer door. Your friends will be amazed, and trailering will be a breeze. It is a skill worth practicing.

There are many steps to this.

- Start with teaching to release the poll.
- Get a solid back up.
- Make sure they can send in both directions.
- Make sure they are comfortable "squeezing" between the fence.
- Make sure they can be safely led onto (and back off of) a trailer.

If your horse has struggled with trailering in the past, you'll need to go very slowly and reward every time they try.

Send downhill/uphill

Each incline presents its own set of challenges for a horse and offers a different experience regarding building muscle groups. This is an excellent way to exercise a horse who has been out of work or to exercise a horse when you cannot ride.

- Make sure the hill is dry and not slick.
- Do not stand directly above or below your horse on the hill.
- Eventually, you can position yourself halfway up the hill and lunge in a circle.

Remember that this is hard work for your horse, and be mindful of their fitness before long periods of this exercise.

Send into a ditch

Most horses will attempt to jump the ditch, so try to send them into it, not over it (running down one side and up the other instead of leaping across).

All of the sending exercises help build muscle in the horse and trust in you as a leader. They are encouraged to think about how to move their body in different ways, paying attention to your cues. These exercises also help develop a horse that is safe and respectful on the ground.

Longlining/ground driving

Young horses are often longlined before being ridden to increase their sensitivity to bit cues for direction and to keep them soft and flexible in their body. This encourages the horse to carry themselves correctly before having a rider on their back. The muscles for carrying a rider need to be developed for good balance, and longlining can help.

Longlining is best learned with an experienced helper and a horse who already knows how to do it. Trying to train your horse to longline while learning how to do it yourself is a recipe for disaster.

Before you begin, your horse should be comfortable with ropes around their hindquarters, back legs, and body and understand basic steering.

Outfit your horse with a properly fitted bit, bridle/headstall, and a saddle

or a surcingle (like a full-body cinch with metal rings). You also need driving reins, or you can use two 22-foot lead ropes.

- Run the lead ropes through the stirrups on your saddle or the surcingle's topmost ring. Connect them to the bit.
- Start slowly, at the walk.
- Position yourself on the driveline, and send your horse forward by wiggling both lines, stepping forward, and saying, "Walk on."
- Let your horse walk forward, even if they do not initially bend in a circle. You want them to understand that forward is the correct direction.
- Gradually ask them to come into a circle by gently bumping the inside line. Do not pull — ask with a squeeze of the hand holding the inside line.
- Keep contact on both lines the same. If the outside line goes slack, they are turning their head out of the circle. If the inside line goes slack, they are falling into the circle with their body (dropping their shoulder).
- The goal is a balanced bend in the body, indicated by even pressure on the lines.
- Turn to the opposite direction by applying pressure to the outside lead rope.

Troubleshooting

- If your horse does not stand for ropes on their body, go back to desensitizing first.
- Reinforce any turning requests with a verbal cue or multiple bumps if needed.
- Do not walk directly behind your horse. You may eventually drive from behind (ground driving), especially if you teach them to pull an object or a cart, but starting off to the side is safer as you both learn. You will be in nearly the same position as when you are lunging to start, but eventually you may move a bit closer to their body.
- Again, this is a complicated technique, best learned in the company of an experienced person, with a trained horse, before working with your horse.

Lunge over cavaletti

Cavaletti are wooden ground poles that can be sitting on the ground or slightly raised. They encourage your horse to pick up their feet and drive from behind. Many horses learn to lunge over cavaletti before training for jumping, and many riders do the same. This is good exercise for older horses that drag their feet (front and back). It also helps a horse become more aware of their feet, with the added benefit of building muscle along the top line.

- Space cavaletti between three and seven feet. This distance varies depending on the size of your horse and the gait.
- Start with one or two poles set in a straight line.
- Slowly increase the space between the poles to encourage a longer stride length, or ask for more strides as you collect.

Some variations

- Arrange cavaletti in a fan shape. This encourages them to bend over the poles.

- Lift one end of alternating cavletti slightly to build more strength in the raised side.
- Cavaletti arranged at a random distance encourages your horse to pay attention to where they are putting their feet. It will help them stretch their neck down, round through their back, and pick their feet up (see more exercises using ground poles/cavaletti in chapter 10).
- Begin all these exercises at the walk, then move to the trot and canter as you are ready.

Lunge over jumps

Start with small cross rails, working up to higher and broader jumps. Horses trained in liberty work can lunge over jumps without a halter, but your horse should be well-attuned to you before attempting this.

Your horse needs to be:

- Confident in your leadership
- Good at sending in both directions
- Able to maintain a gait on their own
- Fit enough to jump

Send and change directions

This is a complicated maneuver that gets a horse's mind trained on you, puts together complete control of their body, and increases a horse's respect for you as the leader.

You'll need a horse who can flex laterally and move both the hindquarters and shoulders before you try this.

- Start by sending your horse to the right (lead rope in the right hand, flag or stick/string in the left).
- As they pick up their inside hind leg, release their hindquarters as you switch

the lead rope and flag hands, stepping toward their left shoulder.

- In a perfect world, they rock back on their hindquarters and release the front end, stepping over to the left.
- Send them to the left.
- Repeat, ad infinitum.

There is a lot to organize here. Go slowly and give yourself time to get into the rhythm of the circle each time you change direction. If you see them lower their head and start to lick and chew, let them stop on the circle and rest.

When you get good at this, travel the length of an outdoor arena, walking up the center line and sending your horse in semi-circles in front of you.

Troubleshooting

- If they step towards you when they change direction, make sure you are asking in time with the feet.
- If they continue to step forward, tap their shoulder with a flag or a stick and string.
- If they startle as you swap hands, go back to desensitizing and sending in one direction.

Voice commands

Work on voice commands: whoa, walk, trot, canter. Train this simultaneously as you are teaching your horse to lunge.

Decide what verbal commands you'd like to use and use them consistently when you want something to happen (and only then). One idea is to use a transition-type phrase or sound as you move from one gait to another to let your horse know a change is coming, For example, you can say, from a trot to a walk, "Aaaand...walk," and then from a walk to a halt, "Aaaand HO." The drawn-out "and" signals your horse to slow down without changing gaits, recognizing that they will be downshifting.

Praise when your horse responds, and make sure your body language isn't working against you. Don't verbally ask for the stop when your body is driving them forward.

CHAPTER 4

AT LIBERTY

"Certainly, we need great movers and powerful jumpers, but above all, we need a partner, not a slave. We need horses who are supremely courageous, fiercely independent, and phenomenally agile. Find such a horse and treasure him. Teach them that you will trust him with your life. Give him the education he will need, and then sit quietly while he does the job you have very skillfully and very patiently taught him. He won't let you down. We owe all this and more to our horses. " James Wofford

What is liberty training, and who is it for?

Horses in a herd are either doing something together — eating, playing, walking — or doing nothing (napping, standing and resting, etc.). If you are only ever grabbing your horse out of the field to do something, you are missing one of the best parts of life, and your horse only ever associates you with work.

The Italians have a phrase for this pleasure of doing nothing: la dolce far niete. Some of the best training begins with nothing, just sitting in a field with your horse, enjoying the company of the herd. They may decide to wander over, lay their head in your lap, and take a nap. When they come to you on their own, opting to spend time with you, you are laying the foundation for liberty training.

Liberty training is one of the best tools for developing a strong bond with your horse. Because they are not connected to you with a halter and a lead rope, every movement they make is by their own choice. It becomes a dance, a beautiful give and take, and a lovely way to create a willing and trusting equine partner. Liberty work is great for:

- Young horses just coming into training
- Older horses that need exercise
- Traumatized horses that are shut down or have trust issues
- Horses that cannot be ridden
- Horses that need more mental stimulation
- Riders who want to understand better how their horse thinks
- Riders who want their horse to be happier in their work

In short, liberty work is a great tool for all horses and riders. It builds respect and trust, deepening communication with every interaction you have. You'll start to understand how your horse communicates, and you will become a better listener.

Many people find that liberty work helps address "vices" or "bad" behaviors better than any other type of training. In many cases, vices and unwanted behaviors are created by interactions with humans. When a horse understands that they are free to move and make choices without punishment or aggression, they may naturally drop those habits on the ground and under the saddle.

Some general guidelines

- Your horse is free to leave you at any time.
- The horse should not have any tack on (this includes a halter).
- A horse can say "no" to a request without punishment.

Troubleshooting

- If your horse leaves you more than they stay, that's good information. Slow down, and try again.
- If your horse lives in a large field, bringing them to a smaller paddock to start is okay.
- It's also okay to start with a halter on. This only becomes problematic if you constantly grab the halter or lead rope.
- You can use a dressage whip or thin lunge whip without a cord to reinforce cues, but they are never applied to the horse's body. If you cannot be judicious in using this training aid, it's best to leave it out.

A word about treats

Using treats is a faster way to get results, but proceed with caution. If you have a pushy or mouthy horse, giving treats can lead to unpleasant behaviors. Horses appreciate rest and peace as much as they enjoy treats, but if you do choose to use treats, there are a few guidelines.

- Store treats in an easy-to-reach place (i.e., a fanny pack or loose pocket).
- Make sure their head is straight forward when you give a treat.
- Do not give a treat if the horse is rooting through your pockets or pouch (a.k.a. "mugging" you).
- Once a horse learns a liberty cue, do not give a treat every time.
- Some trainers add a "click" with their tongue as a precursor to clicker training.

The horse begins associating the click with a treat, which becomes its reward.

- Make treats low- or no-sugar, and be mindful of weight gain.

Cheek lead

Contrary to popular belief, liberty training does not mean you will never touch your horse. This first exercise is a good example of that.

Practicing a cheek lead lays the foundation for having your horse walk beside you without a halter or lead rope. It's also helpful to bring a horse in from the field when you forget to grab a halter and lead rope.

- Start on either side of your horse.
- Wrap your hand under their neck and rest your fingertips on their cheek.
- Apply slight pressure in a pulsing action as you step forward.
- Do not press and hold — pulse until they move, then stop and reward. Try a few more steps, eventually with featherlight pressure.

Troubleshooting

- If they are reluctant to step forward, turn their head towards you and take a step to the side to "unstick" their feet.
- Your horse may respond better to pressure on their cheek, or they might prefer you place your hands between their cheek and their nose. Experiment to see where they are most comfortable.
- Practice this from both sides.

Walking at liberty

Before you can move to other types of liberty work, you'll need to get tuned in to your horse (and they need to get curious and focused on you). One of the best ways to do this is to practice walking at liberty.

You can begin this exercise using a cheek lead, then dropping your hand and continuing to walk.

- If possible, time up with your horse's feet so you are stepping on the same foot.
- Stop and reward if using treats, or rest and praise.
- If your horse routinely walks ahead of you and you opt for a training aid, raise the whip in front of you in the hand farthest from your horse until it is perpendicular to the ground, stopping your feet simultaneously.
- Step forward again.
- Remember to practice walking on both sides. Vary your speed and direction.
- If your horse separates from you and walks away, let them wander and wait for them to return.
- Remember that you'll need a clear, confident walk in a specific direction for your horse to follow. They will not follow an insecure leader at liberty.
- Vary your speed and direction. They should stay tuned in at your near shoulder. This is important for more complicated liberty exercises.
- Transition frequently between the walk and the trot.

Backing

Backing a horse is another example of liberty training that uses touch, at least initially. There are three methods to back your horse, all of which lead to a lighter back up that is eventually accomplished with just a change in your energy.

Option A: Hand pressure on the nose

- Stand facing your horse.
- Place your hand on the bridge of your horse's nose.
- Do not squeeze; just add slight pressure while thinking in your mind BACK.
- When they step back, let go.
- Do not increase pressure, and do not let your mind wander.
- Do not follow their nose with your hand when they back.

Option B: Hand pressure on the chest

- Use the same method for backing but with a hand on the chest instead of the nose. Remember to release when they step back, even just one step to begin.
- For really dull, young, or shutdown horses, release when they shift their weight. They may not take a complete step back at first. A quick release is critical in softening a shut-down horse.
- Do not increase pressure.
- Focus on that backward step. This directs your energy and influences how the horse moves.
- Gradually ask for more steps.
- Remember to practice on both sides of the horse.

Option C: Backing beside your horse

Once your horse has the hang of backing up to a hand on their nose or chest, it's time to work on a liberty back up. Although a very attuned horse can complete this way of backing up before working with the nose and chest options, sometimes it's best to work up to this.

- Stand beside your horse, facing the same direction.
- Imagine that your belly button is shining a light backward through your spine. Think BACK.
- Shift your body weight and step back with the foot closest to your horse.
- If your horse understands verbal cues, you can say "back" simultaneously.
- You can also use the dressage whip, tapping the air in front of you as you step back.
- Look for one step, stop, and reward/praise.

Releasing the hind

At liberty, releasing the hind has the same benefits and follows the same basic principles as it does when completed in a halter and lead rope. The difference is that the horse chooses to bend and move their back feet — you are not holding them in a shape by containing their head.

- Start by facing the hind end.
- Reach under their jaw and place your hand like you would for a cheek lead (wherever they prefer).
- Add a slight pulsing pressure to their face or cheek as you walk towards their hind.
- When they release their hind, rub on their cheek to stop.
- If they toss their head to evade the pressure, stay with them.
- Do not increase pressure. Add a rhythmic, steady pulse instead of harder pulling.
- Make sure your entire energy is directed on moving the hip over.

- At first, reward any effort. Eventually, add steps and make sure the inside back foot steps in front of the outside back foot as it crosses.
- Remember to work on both sides. As with any training, you may find that one side is more willing than the other.

Boomerang

The boomerang is a liberty movement that sends your horse away before bringing them back — all without a lead rope or halter. The goal is to get your horse connected enough to return to you, even when their first movement is away.

- Place an object like an upside-down bucket or cone anywhere you are working. Make sure there is plenty of room to move around it.
- Walk your horse to the bucket, then use body language (belly button pointing behind the driveline) and a leading hand to point your horse around the bucket away from you.
- When the bucket or object is almost to the point of their hip, back up and draw them towards you. Imagine your belly button is again shining through your back and pointing the way for them to go.
- If they take even one step in your direction, stop and reward.

Troubleshooting

- If your horse won't circle the bucket without you, work on releasing the hind.
- If your horse doesn't come back to you, work on drawing them to you as a separate movement.
- The hardest part is getting them to come back. You can start this movement with a halter and lead rope if you are struggling. Keep the slack in the rope as you draw them to you, and reward. Alternatively, just slow down, spend time building a bond, and try again.

Liberty work vs. trick training

Liberty work is the deliberate practice of reading, directing, and responding to your horse's body language. It uses simple cues and well-timed rewards to show your horse that you understand their language and consider them a partner (not a beast of burden, subservient to you). Many of the exercises at liberty mirror what horses might do with each other naturally in the wild.

Trick training may start with liberty work, but it's more about asking a horse to perform specific movements on command (i.e., lying down, stepping on a platform). These movements can have practical applications in daily horse care and keeping, and they can undoubtedly demonstrate a level of trust between you and your equine partner. Still, they are not necessarily movements a horse would undertake on their own. Some trick training is also completed with a halter and lead rope (although you can certainly try without it).

Both liberty work and trick training can be very rewarding and are great activities to do with your horse when riding is not an option. You may notice that some horses really enjoy this work while others are going through the motions. That's okay. Recognizing and honoring their preferences is one more way to build a solid relationship.

Circling

Imagine your horse perfectly balanced on the lunge line. All four feet are in harmony, and their body forms a lovely curve from nose to tail, with the inside ear trained on you in the center. Their neck is level (or slightly elevated at the poll), their back is lifted and engaged, and their hindquarters are reaching underneath as they travel in perfect cadence at the walk, trot, and canter.

Now imagine the same beautiful circle at liberty. With small physical cues, your horse tunes into every slight adjustment to travel around you, maintaining their gait for as long as you ask. A slight glance at their inside hindquarters and they release to face you, eyes soft and relaxed.

Sound like a dream? This is the liberty circle, and you can make it happen.

You can begin this work by teaching your horse to lunge correctly. You are not running them in endless circles here, just laying a foundation for your horse for what you expect when you move your body a certain way. Because your body language is so important, it can be helpful to videotape a few sessions (or enlist a knowledgeable friend to watch you) so you can see what happens when you move.

Keep in mind that lunging on or off the lead rope should not consist of you mindlessly chasing your horse in circles until exhaustion (yours or theirs). It's a way to tune in to them and get their mind on you.

To begin:

- Make sure back up and sending cues are solid.
- Practice leading and changing directions, especially with turns towards the inside. If the horse is not following you as you turn, it may be hard to send them out on a circle.
- You may start by training this on a loose lead rope, but only if you do not rely on the lead rope to pull their attention to you.
- Start in the liberty leading position.

- As you lead, slow your footsteps and turn with your shoulders, walking in a smaller circle in the center.
- You begin to move your body less, still asking your horse to continue to move.
- Your horse should be trained to follow your inside shoulder, so their nose should follow as you turn your inside shoulder.
- If your horse starts to move away from you towards the outside of the circle, take a "drawing" stance to bring them back to you.
- If you choose to use a training aid (dressage whip, etc.). Keep it in your outside hand and use it behind you to keep your horse at a steady tempo as needed. Do not overuse this tool. If you rely on it too much, remove the tool.

PART II

RIDING

"...If I have always worked honestly, my horse will carry me to the end of the world."
E.F. Seidler

Even though horses had been in my life for over a decade (and decades longer than that if you count a childhood and adolescence spent wrapped in a cocoon of every horse book I could get my hands on), I took my first official riding lesson on December 1, 2020. As I flopped around the ring, attempting to control my flailing limbs on a saintly lesson horse, I felt freedom even in my frustration and discomfort. The possibility of more with a horse than standing on the ground. A partnership rooted in a balanced seat and quiet hands.

This does not come instantly or easily to any rider at any age. Sure, some people seem immediately comfortable astride, but it's the smaller refinements, not the hands-free jumping and cantering, that make a good rider. The stable, independent seat. The horse that seems to anticipate transitions. The light, fluid connection between horse and rider.

The following chapters contain riding exercises that can be done alone or with an instructor or knowledgeable friend.

As ever, pay attention to your horse, ride the horse you have today, and leave the conversation on a positive note.

CHAPTER 5

SIX BASIC MOVEMENTS UNDER SADDLE

"Take your reins like a flower, not like a stone. Take your horse by your waist and by your seat, not by your hand and never by force. If you do it by force, it is not riding, it is something else." Nuno Oliveira

The Six Basic Movements under saddle get your horse thinking and paying attention to what is being asked. It's that first mounted conversation with them, a way to come together and take the first steps toward a riding partnership. When practiced with care and attention, you'll find that getting to their brain through the movement of their feet translates into a more responsive ride and a happier horse — a willing equine partner.

Some riders skip even the most basic groundwork in the rush to mount their horse and then wonder why every ride seems like a struggle. Before you even consider clambering aboard, check in with your horse. Run through the Six Basic Movements on the ground to see how they respond. Look for soft, attentive eyes; perky ears; and light responses. With practice, this initial groundwork takes less than five minutes and is an easy way to tune into your horse. It's also a way to see where their brain is and to gauge their energy level before you ride.

Once connected with your partner on the ground, it's time to take the next step. You've laid the foundation for better communication. It's time to ride.

Emergency (one-rein) stop

Many English riders are less familiar with a one-rein stop, but it's a great tool to have in your toolbox when a horse is feeling fresh.

Why use a one-rein stop?

Horses who are running away and not listening to simple brake aids may respond to a one-rein stop. Steady pressure on one rein forces them to slow down. It is a rare horse that can continue cantering with their body deeply bent.

Practice this 90-degree lateral flexion at a walk before you need it on the trail or in the ring.

- Walk your horse forward.
- Choose a spot, sit deep in the saddle, and begin to apply pressure to one rein.
- Do not jerk the rein back; slide your hand down towards the bit and apply pressure back towards your hip.
- They should flex to the side with the shorter rein, stopping their feet completely.
- Release the instant their feet stop, but don't throw your rein away or let them rip the reins out of your hand. This bad habit is harder to correct than it is to prevent. Let the release be timely and smooth.

Practice this on both sides at the walk and trot, and let your horse straighten their neck fully between sides.

Troubleshooting

- If your horse continues to turn a circle, crossing their back legs over one another, make sure you are not applying any leg pressure.
- Do not increase pressure if they keep turning. Keep it steady and be patient until their feet stop moving.
- Do not lean forward or shift your seat.
- Once their feet stop moving, release immediately. Timing is everything when you first start.
- Do not apply a one-rein stop on a narrow trail or if your horse runs away at a full canter or gallop. This can throw them off balance and cause an accident. If your horse runs away, try to slow them down by turning smaller circles, applying the one-rein stop as they come back under control.

The importance of "feel"

People who practice natural horse training methods often mention "feeling for the horse" or looking for a certain "feel." In principle, it means a few things.

- *When you reach for a horse, give them time to reach back to you.*
- *Commit to letting your horse try things to figure out what you're asking.*
- *Use the lightest cue possible and reward the slightest try.*
- *Recognize and reward softness in your horse's response.*

Only through regular work with our horses can we cultivate feel, and only then can we truly elevate our relationships with these beautiful creatures.

Backing

Backing under saddle is a perfect opportunity to practice tuning in to your horse's feel. This is not a common movement for your horse, but it's good exercise for their body and mind.

- Take up contact in the reins. Relax your seat.
- Apply even backward pressure. Do not pull or jerk.
- Keep your legs off their sides.
- Pay attention to their body and their ears. If they shift their weight back or soften into the bridle, release the pressure and pause.
- Take up contact again. Release again when they respond.
- The faster you release when they get it right, the less pressure you will need to get the response you are looking for.
- Apply pressure again and ask for a step. Release when their foot lands.
- Continue to add steps until all four feet have moved, then build from there.

The eventual goal is a light, timely response of as many steps as you ask for with a level, relaxed head (or a slightly elevated poll).

Troubleshooting

- If they move forward, make sure you are not applying leg pressure.
- If they brace against the contact, add a light, rhythmic pulse to it until they shift their weight or move their feet.
- If they throw their head in the air, try for lighter contact to start.
- If your horse struggles with this and gives just one good step or shift back, stop there.

Releasing the hindquarters

Releasing the hindquarters is also referred to as turning on the forehand. The horse's front feet remain planted as their inside hind foot steps across and in front of their outside hind and their butt swings around in a circle.

This maneuver combines lateral flexion with seat and leg cues. Flexion to approximately 90 degrees must happen before you can ask for them to release and swing their hindquarters around. It's easiest to start at a halt.

- Make sure your horse is standing balanced and square.
- If you start with the horse releasing their hindquarters to the left, ask for lateral flexion to the right. Pull the right rein with steady contact open slightly and back towards your hip.
- As they flex, tap them with your right heel just behind the girth.
- At first, any step of their hindquarters is correct. Release and reward.
- Eventually, you'll want the inside back leg to step in front of the outside back leg. You'll feel this as your inside hip drops slightly.
- As you progress, you can combine this with circles. Walk in a circle, release the hindquarters for a step or two, then get back on the circle.
- Practice in both directions, and give your horse plenty of time to straighten their neck and relax between sides.

Troubleshooting

- If your horse moves forward, keep steady contact on the rein that is not flexing their neck laterally. Do not simply pull backward — redirect the energy where you want it.
- If they do not respond to the heel tap, continue with steady rein pressure and tapping until they move.
- For experienced horses that are not responding (or are dull), you can increase the intensity of the tap until they release. Immediately stop once they respond with even the slightest step.

Release shoulders

Some horses are naturally heavier on the forehand, so releasing their shoulders to turn on their haunches can be challenging (even more so with a rider aboard). To complete it, you'll combine slight lateral flexion, backing, and releasing the front feet to move around the pivoting back inside foot.

- To start with a step to the left, you must ask when the front left is leaving the ground.
- Start by establishing flexion to 45 degrees with the inside rein, then add a slight movement back with the outside rein.
- Back a few steps, then when the left foot leaves the ground, open the left rein and apply the right leg at the girth (or slightly behind) to ask your horse to step over to the left.
- If they step over, release and reward.
- The correct movement sees the outside front leg stepping in front of the inside foot, with the inside hind foot planted as a pivot. This refinement can take a while, so ask for one step at a time and then get more precise over time.
- Work this movement in both directions.

Troubleshooting

- Starting this movement from the back up means your horse won't naturally try to go forward, but you can also start from a halt. Take up contact on the reins to help your horse shift their weight back from the forehand, then proceed to ask for a step to the side.
- If your horse walks forward, stop, back a few steps, and try again.
- If your horse does not step over, add slight leg pressure, but do not overbend or pull in the direction you want the shoulders to go. You want their attention in that direction but not full lateral flexion.

Riding squares

Another excellent exercise to reinforce shoulder movement and prevent a horse from dropping its shoulder when turning is to ride squares. Practicing five or ten feet from the rail also supports straightness, balance, and a good square halt.

- Walk along the rail to about five feet from the next fence and halt.
- Move the shoulders over from the halt, one step at a time, until your horse has made a 90-degree turn.
- Repeat this movement at each corner, halting first and then giving the cue to move the shoulders over.
- Master this in one direction (your horse's best side) before moving to the other.

If turning from a halt is too much to ask and your horse needs a little momentum to get going, start the square turn earlier, and ask them to move their shoulders over when the outside foreleg leaves the ground.

Eventually, you can make the square smaller and smaller and ask for a horse to do it at a trot, but don't try to change it up too much at once. Let them figure it out at a slower gait first, then build from there.

Backing in a circle

When backing in a circle, you are learning to make your horse's steps more precise and aiming them in a direction. You are also:

1. Helping a distracted horse to focus
2. Building strength and suppleness in the shoulders
3. Developing balance throughout your horse's body

Here's how to do it.

- Begin by asking your horse to back a few steps.
- Once they have the backward motion, open the outside rein slightly to tip their nose to the outside of the circle.
- Keep your outside leg on slightly behind the girth. The inside leg stays at the girth.

Troubleshooting

- If your horse throws their head in the air when you ask them to back, slow down and ask with less pressure.
- If they turn to the outside, use less rein pressure.
- If they don't release back, don't hang on their mouth. Add a few rhythmic bumps with the reins until they become unstuck, releasing with each step or backward movement.
- Don't ask for too much to start. Get a few good steps, then end on a high note.
- If they cannot understand what you are asking, work more on backing and releasing the hind and shoulders. Get light and timely in this movement, then try again.

CHAPTER 6

DEVELOP AN INDEPENDENT SEAT

"An old adage says that a good rider can hear his horse speak and a great rider can hear his horse whisper." Elizabeth Letts

An independent seat is the key to an enjoyable, safe ride for you and your equine partner. When you are balanced and moving well over your horse's constantly changing center of gravity, your horse can relax and not worry that you'll suddenly kick them or grab at their mouth. Taking the time to learn how to balance also means you'll be ready for anything that comes up in the ride.

Start with easy stretches at the halt before progressing to more challenging movements in motion. Some of these exercises require help, while others can be completed independently on or off the horse (and at many different gaits).

You'll need:

- A horse experienced in lunging, especially in transitioning between gaits
- An instructor or experienced friend to help
- Courage and a willingness to try

It starts with a deep seat

One main challenge is understanding what it feels like to sit deep in the saddle. Many new riders feel perched atop their moving creature — a precarious position that causes them to jerk at the reins and become more nervous.

To really sit deep, you'll need a leg rotated from the hip socket so that the entire inside of your leg is in contact with the horse.

You'll also need to feel the sitting bones making equal contact. Before moving your legs into the correct position, sit in the saddle and focus on your sitting bones. Can you feel where they make contact in the saddle? If not:

- Lean forward slightly and move the flesh of your buttocks to the side. Sit back.
- Lengthen down through the front and back of your body. Imagine your pelvis straight up and down, held up by a long, tall spine.
- Engage the muscles of the core slightly — don't clench.
- Take a few steps focusing on your sitting bones.
- If you cannot quite feel them, don't worry. This noticing takes practice and time.

Another way to feel your sitting bones is to drop your stirrups and bring both knees towards your horse's withers (engage your core to help). This movement rocks you back and can help highlight any (im)balance of your seat bones while sliding you deeper into the saddle. When you release, try to keep your seat bones where they are.

Move your attention to your legs. If you glance down and your toes are pointing out (or your stirrup irons are not perpendicular to your horse), chances are good the back of your calf is hugging the horse. This rotates your entire body up out of the saddle (and means your leg is less effective).

To correct this:

- Starting with the left leg, take your foot out of the stirrup and let it hang briefly.
- Lift the leg straight out to the side.
- Rotate your left heel slightly outwards while moving your knee back and down.
- Notice how the leg feels against the side of the horse.
- Maintain this position as you take up the stirrup again.

- Repeat this movement on the right side.

If you aren't sure your horse will stand still for this, have someone hold them while you make adjustments.

Ride bareback

Riding bareback remains one of the best ways to feel your horse's movement underneath you. You don't need a fancy pad, but if your horse has a bony spine or tall withers, a simple pad can make it more comfortable for both of you. Take a walk along a trail for even more connection (and a nice break from work in the ring).

Barrel challenge

Not sure how your balance is to begin with? Try the barrel challenge.

Find an empty rain barrel (or some other sturdy barrel that can support your weight), and place your saddle on it. Mount the saddle and put your feet in the stirrups. If you feel steady, add some motion.

- Move into two-point.
- Raise your arms over your head, out to the sides, and behind your back.
- Twist to one side, then another.
- Post a "trot."

As you do this, notice what happens to your feet and legs. Do your knees and heels come up, or do they stay long and stable? What muscles engage your buttocks and core to keep the barrel upright?

All this is good information you can use when you get on your horse.

Stationary lunge line lessons

The exercises below are suitable for stretching your body before a ride and learning to plug your seat bones into the saddle. They can be done at the walk, too, but be mindful if you're navigating the horn of a western saddle. Better yet? Try them bareback.

Touch ears

- Lean forward with each hand to touch your horse's ears/poll.
- Try to keep your seat bones connected to the saddle.
- Focus on lengthening your spine to reach, not stretching your shoulder.

Touch toes on both sides

- This helps stretch out your legs and back.
- It's helpful when you need to re-position your foot in the stirrup.
- Keep your balance in the saddle and lean over to touch each foot.
- Keep your core engaged, especially if your lower back is tight or sensitive.

Left hand to horse's right shoulder

- This exercise increases flexibility and strength in your torso.
- Inhale to lift your arms above your head as you stretch your legs down.

- Exhale, pulling your navel to your spine and twisting to the right, reaching for your horse's shoulder.
- Stay in the twist for a couple of breaths.
- To come up, take a deep breath, exhale, and lift your torso up.
- Repeat with the right hand to your horse's left shoulder.
- Work into this gradually, and do not strain to reach.

Touch rump

- Twist to each side to touch your horse's rump.
- Move with your breath, inhaling to stretch tall and exhaling to twist.
- Hold each twist for a few seconds.
- You can also twist in time with each inhale and exhale.
- This is another great way to work on desensitizing your horse's hindquarters.

Lunge line lessons in motion

If you are a new rider (or a less confident returning rider), working with an instructor on the lunge line can help. The instructor controls the speed and direction of a trustworthy horse, so all you need to do is relax and work to absorb the movement.

Starting on a lunge line helps develop a balanced, independent seat. Because you don't have to worry about steering or speed, you can focus entirely on seat and strength.

Practice walk—>trot—>walk transitions

- Start by establishing a good walking rhythm.
- Hold your hands in a regular rein position.
- Have the person lunging use verbal cues to prepare you to move to a trot, then back to a walk and halt.

- Practice in both directions.
- Continue with these transitions until you feel comfortable.
- Challenge yourself by raising your arms above your head or straight out to the sides as you ride the transitions.
- You can also add ground poles and either sit or post the trot.
- Drop your stirrups to really test your seat and balance.

Practice trot—>canter—>trot transitions

- This is a great way to get more comfortable at the canter.
- In the beginning, hold the mane or the horn of your western saddle.
- Stretch long through your legs and sit deep to follow your horse's motion.
- Lightly engage the core without tightening the hips.
- Work towards a hands-free transition between the trot and the canter.
- You may feel unbalanced and tense at first; with practice, you will learn to relax, which will relax your horse.

Airplane arms

- Put your arms straight out to the sides in the shape of a T.
- Ride on the lunge at a walk, a trot and, eventually, a canter.
- To make it more challenging, close your eyes.
- At the walk, call out which foot is hitting the ground and when.
- This exercise helps you better feel the movement of your horse.

Airplane arms with a twist

- Start in airplane arms.
- Inhale, then as you exhale, twist to one side.
- Inhale to come back to the center; exhale to the other side.

- Follow the rhythm of your horse's gait.
- Keep your shoulders relaxed, the sides of your body long, core engaged.
- Practice at the trot in both directions.

Triangle pose on horseback

Combine a major stretch with core activation and balance with triangle pose on horseback. Bring your arms into the shape of a T. Make sure your lower belly is engaged. Inhale deeply, and twist to the left on an exhale, pulling your navel to your spine.

Take a deep breath in, lengthening the crown of your head to the sky, then on an exhale, extend your torso forward and pivot the arms down so that the back of your right hand presses into your horse's left shoulder as your left hand extends to the sky.

On each inhale, reach down through your heels, back through your seat bones, and forward with the crown of your head. Pull your navel into your spine on each exhale and open your heart to the sky. Your lower body may resemble a two-point position. Keep the muscles in your waist engaged to maintain balance and not collapse out of the saddle.

Rise up on an exhale by backing out the way you came into this, or simply exhale and bring your left hand to meet your right, resting on your horse's neck for a few breaths. Repeat on the other side.

This can be practiced at a standstill first, but challenge yourself to do it on the lunge while the horse is in motion. Twist towards the inside of the circle.

Arms above your head

- Inhale and stretch your arms above your head.
- Relax your shoulders.
- Deepen your seat.
- Stretch your heels down.
- Engage your core.
- Use this exercise to better feel which foot is moving. When a hip drops, the hind foot on the dropping side leaves the ground.
- Practice at all gaits in both directions.

Riding for balance

The first two exercises can also be completed on the lunge line but can also be practiced on your own.

Post without reins

- Tie the reins in a knot and then let them go.
- Position your hands as if you were holding reins.
- Do not squeeze with your knees.
- Use your core muscles to push your pelvis forward and rise slightly out of the saddle.
- Push your heels down as your pelvis moves forward.

Post and canter without stirrups

- Drop your stirrups.
- Establish a steady rhythm at the trot.
- Use your core strength and your quads and hamstrings to lift you up and slightly forward in the saddle.
- You may feel pressure at the back of your knee, but do not pinch with the knee to rise out of the saddle.
- The movement won't be dramatic — think a slight forward-moving lift in time with the outside front leg rather than a big rise out of the saddle.
- When this is comfortable, sit and ask for a canter.

One-handed trot

This exercise helps you stretch down through your leg and balance yourself over your horse's center without relying on the reins.

- Establish a rhythmic posting trot.

- Place the inside hand on your hip joint and put the reins in your outside hand.
- Use leg and seat cues to ride a large figure eight, switching the hand on the hip and the reins as you turn so that the reins are always in your outside hand.
- Your hip points should turn in the direction you want your horse to travel. Your outside shoulder will naturally come forward slightly. Make sure not to drop your inside shoulder as you turn.

Cone bending

- Set up a line of cones down the straight center line.
- Practice weaving in and out of the cones using only seat and leg cues.
- This can be done without reins and stirrups, too, at all gaits (eventually!).
- Consider this the first phase of training for barrel racing, where the most accomplished racers need only add seat and leg cues to bend their horse around a barrel.

Counting challenge

Part 1

Challenge yourself in the posting to trot to rise for two beats, then sit for two beats. If you need to rest your hands on your horse's neck to avoid pulling on their mouth, grab some mane. The balance will come.

Part 2

Same challenge, except this time you'll rise for two beats and sit for one.

Part 3

Same challenge, except you'll remain standing in your stirrups for a lap or two around the ring. This is great for your core, hamstrings, and ankles. Staying connected to your core muscles while letting your ankles and hips absorb the shock of the trot is key.

Part 4

Once you have the first three parts down, it's time to add more movement. This not only helps you develop balance; it also positions your legs correctly underneath you and strengthens your back and your hamstrings.

- Start this at the halt, then progress to the walk and (maybe) the trot and canter.
- Come into a two-point position with weight spilling into your lower legs and heels as your seat lifts out of the saddle.
- Grab some mane to help you balance.
- Slowly count to four as you rise to stand in the stirrups.
- Lengthen your heels and straighten your knees and hips.

- Pause. Get your balance.
- Reverse the count and slowly lower back to two-point position.
- From two-point, count to four as you stretch your arms toward your horse's ears and lower your chest onto their neck. Your legs and hips stay in two-point — press your navel to your spine to steady yourself.
- Pause.
- Reverse the count to rise back to two-point position.

Try this at the walk. Make sure to follow the movement of your horse's head with soft hands and loose arms. You can also speed up (or slow) the rate of counting, but keep it consistent.

Figure 4 stretch with high lunge

If you are still struggling to open your hips for a deeper, more independent seat, you're not alone. Years of sitting at a desk or in the car result in tight hips with a limited range of motion.

But sometimes, one simple stretch can help. Try a Figure 4 stretch just before you mount.

- *Stand about arm's distance away from your tacked horse on their near side. You need enough room to bring your knee to hip height.*
- *Take a deep breath in, and on an exhale, lift your left knee to hip height. Place your hands on your horse for balance.*
- *Take another deep breath, then rotate your left knee out to place your left ankle on your right knee. You should feel a big stretch in the outside left hip (and maybe some sensation on the inside of your left thigh).*
- *If you want to go deeper, slowly bend your right knee so you sit back. Let your sitting bones reach for an imaginary chair behind you.*
- *Wherever you are, take five full, deep, even breaths, then press into your right leg to*

straighten and release your left ankle.

- *Move to the other side of your horse and repeat with your right leg.*
- *If your horse is antsy and doesn't want to stand for this, feel free to stretch holding onto a fence or stall door.*

High lunge is another good hip warm-up.

- *Face your horse with your hands on your hips.*
- *Take a deep breath in, lifting your right knee up so it's perpendicular to your hip.*
- *Exhale, and slowly hinge at the hips and swing the right knee back and down, landing with yur right foot behind you so you are in a deep lunge.*
- *Take 5-10 deep breaths, then come out of the pose in the opposite order, exhaling to bring your knee back and through to standing.*
- *Repeat on the other side.*

CREW

CHAPTER 7

TRANSITIONS BETWEEN THE GAITS

"The fastest way to get somewhere is to take your time." Janne Rumbough

Transitions are the unsung heroes of all mounted work. A smooth, stable stop or acceleration in the gaits feels good to both horse and rider.

But too often, riders rush through these moments of change. This can cause your horse to lose their balance and may unseat you in the faster gaits. Proper transitions look like:

- No change in how the horse is carrying themselves in an upward transition (walk-trot-canter)
- A slight lift in the front end as the horse slows between gaits (canter-trot-walk-stop)

Riding properly through this means maintaining an independent seat that helps your horse move through the gaits with balance and ease (more on an independent seat in Chapter 6).

Practicing transitions helps you get a better feel of your horse's movement and improves a horse's responsiveness. Transitions encourage a horse to pay attention to the rider and increases your horse's suppleness and balance. They relax the horse by letting them know what's expected (and who's the leader), and this helps you develop a better relationship with your horse.

Some guiding principles

- Use your breath as a pre-cue for your horse. This lets them know a change is going to occur.
- Cues for transitions follow an order of aids: seat, legs, hands. You may need to apply all three to get the desired result, but remember to move in that order.
- Slightly close your hands on the reins as another pre-cue (a half-halt in English riding).
- Use common sense when trying these exercises. Go slowly.
- If you are nervous and unsure of your horse or ability, do not try these alone. Seek help from a qualified instructor.
- Do not push yourself if you feel you aren't ready. Safety first!
- Aim for eventually getting a light response with fewer cues.
- Reward every try, and don't add pressure too quickly, especially if your horse does not understand.

All this work can be done starting at the walk until it feels effortless. This may seem elementary, but if you can't pull it off at the walk, you'll struggle between faster gaits.

On fear

Fear can be a significant issue for riders of all skill levels. It can hold us back from trying new things or advancing in our riding. For example, many people are scared to canter — they feel unsteady and out of control. This can cause rider error that makes the horse anxious, too. Fear is a natural (and often life-preserving) biological response, but it can become overwhelming if not addressed.

There are a few things that you can do to begin to manage your fear.

- *First, admit your fear without shame. It's okay to be scared.*
- *Be patient. Building confidence takes time.*
- *Learn to ride on a steady, balanced horse. This may not be your horse — taking lessons on a forgiving lesson horse is a good idea.*
- *Start with a solid foundation. Everything you need to learn can start at the walk.*

Don't compare your progress to another rider's. It doesn't matter where other people are in their journey. Your path won't look like anyone else's. You'll have a better time with your horse if you focus on yourself.

In the end, riding is supposed to be enjoyable. Sure, as you advance in your skills, there may be times when you are nervous or even scared to do something. This is what it feels like when you move out of your comfort zone to learn something new.

But forcing yourself to do something when you are terrified does you no good and does your horse no good either.

Transitions with seat cues

Seat cues indicate the transition by using the rider's weight and pressure on the seat bones.

Downward transitions

- On an exhale, weigh your seat down as you lift your lower back.
- Sit back on your pockets, but think of your chest as lighter. You encourage the horse to continue moving into the transition, not to lurch to a sudden halt.
- Bring your energy way down, exhaling audibly and slowing the movement of your hips.
- Soften, and resist the urge to pull back on the reins, even if they do not respond immediately.
- Turning in a circle is another way to help with downward transitions.
- Practice walk to stop, trot to walk to stop, then canter to trot to walk to stop.

Upward transitions

- Leg cues often accompany upward transitions, but moving up through the gaits applying only your seat is possible.
- Make sure your horse feels balanced and responsive at whatever gait you're in — your next gait is only as good as the previous one.
- On an inhale, shift the weight of your seat slightly to the outside. For a canter,

your outside leg might also move backward slightly — this cues your horse to push from behind.

- Lengthen the legs down.
- Move your hands slightly forward to give your horse room to stretch into the upward gait. This is especially important in the canter, where the first step should be up and forward.

Troubleshooting

- If your horse throws their head up (or shoves it down) on downward transitions, you're using too much rein pressure.
- If your horse throws their head up (or shoves it down) on upward transitions, ask with less leg pressure.
- If your horse does not respond to seat cues for upward transitions, add a light squeeze of the inside lower leg.
- If your horse throws their head up and you're not using the reins, your seat may be unbalanced.
- If your horse moves into the upward transition and then immediately slows, you may be grabbing the reins for balance.

Transitions with leg cues

Leg cues are the next level and may be used in quick succession, especially when working with an inexperienced horse. They should be subtle and as light as possible.

- As with everything, reward the slightest try in the beginning.
- Make sure you are clear about what you want before you ask. This makes your cues more clear.
- Think of your legs as a funnel. Push your horse through the funnel to move forward. Use different parts and pressures of leg to move the horse laterally, too.

Leg cue for halt—>walk

- Start from a square halt (see sidebar).
- Stretch your legs down evenly.
- Look forward.
- Apply even pressure with both legs.
- Follow the walk with your hands and seat.
- Keep your elbows soft and flexible (but close to your sides

Practicing the halt

A square halt is more complex than it sounds. Essentially, your horse is evenly balanced, with each leg like a corner post on their body. Many horses struggle with this because their riders rush through the halt into the next activity.

To give your horse ample opportunity to "square up," start with this practice on the ground before moving to mounted work. Halt, square up, and stay there. Let them rest as a reward when he is standing square.

Leg cue for walk—>trot

- Make sure the walk is well-established.
- Keep both legs at the girth/cinch.
- Apply both legs evenly.
- For posting trot, rise when the outside front leg moves forward.
- For sitting trot, engage your core muscles and lengthen both legs down. Imagine your feet walking on the ground on either side of your horse.

Leg cue for trot —>canter

- Look for a well-established and forward trot before asking for a canter.
- It can be helpful to ask for this transition coming out of a corner.
- Sit deep as you apply the leg aids.
- The inside leg stays steady at the girth.
- The outside leg comes just behind the girth.
- As the outside hind leg leaves the ground (your outside hip will drop), apply the inside and outside leg as above.
- The inside rein can come slightly open.
- Apply the leg, seat, and rein aids at the same time: sit, inside, outside, canter.

Troubleshooting

- Some horses are very sensitive to leg cues and lunge forward at even the lightest touch. To work with this, practice keeping your leg on consistently so they understand that every movement doesn't mean "go faster."
- Some horses are dulled to leg pressure. In this case, use leg only when you mean it, and reinforce with additional pressure if they don't respond. On the other side of that coin? Release immediately when they do what you ask. Timing is everything when softening a dull horse.

- If your horse does not canter when you ask, make sure your cues are clear and consistent.
- With time, you can add more challenging transitions, such as going from a halt to a canter.

Riding without a bridle

Riding without reins by using your body to cue your horse requires practice and sensitivity from both horse and rider.

As with all work, you won't simply take your bridle off and expect to guide your horse around with the power of your mind (although wouldn't that be nice!); first, you will see how your horse responds to you with reins in hand (but cueing only with your body), then with reins loose, then with a neck rope, then with nothing but you.

These exercises may be more successful if completed bareback, but you can certainly work on this with a saddle if that makes you feel more secure.

CWD

CHAPTER 8

RIDING EXERCISES

"A horse can lend its rider the speed and strength he or she lacks – but the rider who is wise remembers it is no more than a loan." Pam Brown

You don't need to master the Six Movements under saddle or have perfection in the transitions to start adding riding exercises. Combined with regular transition work between the gaits, these exercises improve the mental and physical health of both horse and rider. In fact, changing up your routine can be helpful for your horse. It keeps them thinking and attentive because they are less able to predict what you're going to ask for when you head out for a ride.

That being said, it's not helpful to be erratic. You can vary the type of work you do, but stay consistent with how you ask.

Remember to:

- Reward the slightest try, especially if it's a new skill or exercise.
- Go slow to go fast. Slowing down gives you and your horse time to think and to experience success together.

Ride in half-seat and two-point

Riding a few laps in half-seat and two-point is an excellent balancing practice for the rider. These two seats are also used in various activities, such as jumping and cantering. Try both during your warm-up at the walk and the trot.

Half-seat

- This is sometimes referred to as a "light" seat.
- Your legs are still in contact with the horse, and your bottom is lightly in the saddle. Your clothes are making contact, but your seat bones are not.
- Your torso is slightly inclined forward as your heels stretch down.
- Half-seat allows you to use your weight a bit more if needed. For example, if you are approaching a jump and need more impulsion, you can still use your weight and legs to ask for more energy from behind.
- Too much energy? Sinking back just a little will slow the movement down.

Two-point

- In two-point, your entire pelvis is out of the saddle. The only points making contact are your knees.

- Stretch down through your heels.
- Reach your hands forward and up your horse's neck.
- Point your seat bones back behind you.
- This seat is used for jumping, with the bottoms of your feet stretching towards the jump as you push your hands up your horse's neck and shine your seat bones behind you.

Serpentines

Serpentines are like a snaky path winding across the arena. They can be subtle and barely off a straight line, or they can be as steep as switchbacks. Think of the track a snake makes across a sandy path — that smooth, even undulation is what you are looking for. This is a great exercise to work on timing your cues with your horse's feet.

- Start anywhere in the ring or arena.
- Pick a spot in your mind to turn your horse before you start to cue.

- Cue first by turning your attention and your body in the direction you'd like to go. This simple movement in the saddle might be enough. This encourages your horse to relax and curve their body into the turn.

To turn your horse, use the proper seat and rein positions. These are for direct-reined horses — neck-reined horses have different rein cues but can be supported with the same leg positions. Some disciplines use slightly different placement of leg cues; western riding uses an inside leg position that is back farther to encourage a horse's barrel to bend deeply around the leg.

Ultimately it's what works for you and your horse, but the placement is roughly the same.

- Inside leg at or slightly behind girth
- Outside leg at girth
- Inside rein flexes in the direction of travel
- Outside rein keeps the horse steady and stays close to the neck
- Add a nudge with the inside leg and open the inside rein if your horse does not begin to turn.
- To switch the direction of travel, start by moving your attention, then adjust your leg position, and then add rein pressure. You can also add a half-halt before even switching your attention. This cues your horse that something is changing and gives them an opportunity to get ready.

Troubleshooting

- If your horse feels stiff or stuck, practice more lateral flexion to warm up.
- If your horse turns abruptly, use less rein pressure.
- If your horse stops, apply more leg pressure.
- Always start this at the walk.
- Add cones for visual direction.

- After they understand what you're asking, add ground poles to encourage your horse to pick up their feet.

Conditioning for horse and rider

While feeling a little sore after vigorous activity is normal, you don't want to end every ride limping back to the barn (you or your horse!). Your time together will be infinitely more enjoyable if you do some conditioning together. This includes:

- *Walking and trotting uphill (hill work)*
- *Long trotting or cantering*
- *Yoga (on and off the horse)*

Chapter 10 has more ideas for exercises on the lunge line and under saddle to improve your horse's fitness.

Large circles to small circles (spiral in)

Circling is a great tool for keeping your horse light in the front end, supple in the body, and moving at the speed you want them to travel. Getting them to respond to your aids to produce a balanced circle can be challenging, but it's work worth doing for all the benefits.

- Start with a larger circle.
- Direct your attention to the center of the circle.
- The cues are essentially the same as the serpentine, except you'll add more leg pressure and rein direction.
- As you circle, gradually spiral in by asking your horse to step their inside back leg in front of the outside back leg (releasing the hind).
- Keep the outside rein against their neck and the inside rein open.
- Once they reach the spiral's center, release their hindquarters and let them rest at a stop. Walk straight before circling in the other direction.

- When you are smooth and confident at the walk, move up to the trot, both posting and sitting.

Troubleshooting

- Do not pull back on the reins to move their head. Think instead about opening the rein like you would open the door for them to step through.
- If your horse pushes their shoulder towards the center of the circle, try to apply pressure with your inside leg as their outside front leg is leaving the ground.
- Proper timing encourages them to stretch into the outside rein and create more of an arc with their body from nose to tail.
- If they push their shoulder too far outside the circle or drift out, add more outside leg pressure just behind the girth and steady the outside rein.
- Be mindful that a small circle at the trot or canter is harder on your horse's joints. Use your best judgment about how small is too small for your horse.

Small circle to large circle (spiral out)

- Reverse the process from a hindquarter release back to a larger circle.
- Start by releasing your horse's hindquarters, gradually opening the inside rein and softening your leg cue to spiral out.
- Add leg pressure from both legs, with the outside leg just behind the girth.
- Do this in both directions, and be aware that one direction is usually more challenging.

Snowman

This more complicated riding exercise requires horse and rider comfort in the trot and the canter in both directions. This activity reinforces your work on circles and your transitions between gaits.

Snowman also:

1. Builds fitness in horse and rider
2. Improves suppleness
3. Helps your horse pick up the correct lead in the canter

Snowman consists of a trotted circle for the head and a cantered one for the body.

- Start by trotting a circle. Establish a steady rhythm and make sure your horse is paying attention.
- Transition to a canter where the "head" of the snowman (your trotted circle) connects with the body (the cantered circle).
- Canter a large circle to form the body, then transition to a trot where the head and body connect. Ride the smaller circle of the head, then transition back to a canter for the body circle.
- Make sure to ride your snowman in both directions.

Troubleshooting

- This can also be completed as a walk/trot snowman at first to establish where the transition occurs.
- Your transitions may be clunky at first. Start by establishing a trot—>canter transition in a simple circle before trying it on the snowman.
- If your horse stumbles as they change gaits, make sure you are balanced in the seat before you ask.
- Don't worry about cantering on the correct lead at first.
- Eventually, you'll want to cue for the correct lead. Time your cue so that you ask when the front leg you want leading is leaving the ground. For example, if you want a right lead canter, cue as the right leg leaves the ground.

Walk to canter figure eight

This is a more advanced exercise to help you develop a feel for changing leads (and a secure seat when skipping the trot transition directly into the canter). A horse that can move into this challenging transition without leaping forward and throwing their head up is more balanced and safe for the rider.

Before introducing this activity, your horse should be able to:

- Move into a canter from leg cues
- Give in the bridle to poll pressure

Use a figure eight pattern to teach this transition. Canter a large circle, walk across the center line (where the two circles of the figure eight would connect), and then pick up your canter on the other lead to make the second circle.

Troubleshooting

- Maintain legs in the canter position (inside leg at the girth, outside leg slightly behind).
- Leg yield off the inside leg when you land in the walk.
- There should be no trot steps.
- The canter should come from behind and be active.
- If it's not working, start in a smaller circle at the canter and get your horse moving well before dropping to a walk and trying again.

In dressage, this is a second-level transition that is completed in a three-loop serpentine. Even if you aren't aiming to develop a Grand Prix mount, this exercise is fun and beneficial for you and your horse.

Walk-lope transition

Some Western disciplines also have a walk-lope transition that starts with the horse backing a few steps, gathering themselves on their hocks, and loping off.

Practicing this transition is good for helping yur horse move off the leg better (and developing your own balance without grabbing the reins when they do). Some cowboys teach this movement while working cattle, but others on a green horse might want the security of a round pen.

Even though many canter or lope cues are given when rounding a corner, this might not be the best way to move up from a walk to a lope. Especially if your horse struggles with tight lateral flexion, practice this tricky transition along the straight edge of a fence before moving into a circle.

Long trotting (or cantering)

In lessons, short periods of trot when warming up gets the muscles loose but doesn't really condition the horse. Take some time a couple of times a week to work on sessions of long trotting or cantering. This is simply trotting or cantering for five to ten minutes at a time, working in changes of direction and switching from posting to sitting trot.

- Allow your horse to stretch long and low, then ask them to come into a more collected trot.
- Post on the "incorrect" lead for a minute or two. Endurance riders do this to keep their horses balanced over distances.
- Mix it up to keep your horse engaged, but focus on going for an extended period.
- When trotting and cantering, make sure to move in both directions equally. Keep track of the time.
- Start with just a few minutes at a time. As you both get more fit, increase either intensity or duration — not both at the same time.

CHAPTER 9

TRY SOMETHING NEW

"For a human to win, it is not necessary for a horse to lose. You should not have to take things away from a horse or break him into fragments in order to train him; rather you should add to the horse. The goal should be making, not breaking." Cherry Hill

It's a strange contradiction that although horses tend to thrive on routine, they also enjoy breaking out of the same old patterns. You might consider trying something new if your horse:

- Seems unwilling to do ring work
- Runs the other way when you gather them in the pasture
- Has a generally poor attitude towards work that cannot be attributed to illness or pain

Some horses may take to new surroundings and activities immediately, while others need more preparation. If you are just starting your journey together, take the time to help your horse feel more confident on your new adventure. Get to know what they need to feel comfortable in your leadership, and they will be a more willing and enthusiastic participant as you explore new things together.

Take lessons

Taking lessons can build confidence, especially if you are an older beginning rider or haven't been in the saddle for a while. To get started, you'll need a few things.

Riding gear

- A helmet: Purchase this new and ASTM-certified. Helmets have an expiration date, so check the tag to make sure it is no more than five years old.
- Riding clothes: Western riders usually wear jeans, but English riders might want to find breeches. Full-seat breeches offer more "stick" and are helpful if you're feeling unbalanced.
- Boots: You don't need to break the bank on boots. Look for anything with a half-inch heel that is comfortable.

A good instructor

"Good" is a relative term. Some riders like the drill sergeant approach to learning, while others prefer a gentler style. Ask to watch a lesson if you are unsure about your instructor's methods.

Regardless of their style, you'll need an instructor who:

- Tailors private lessons to your needs
- Is professional (on time, courteous, not on their phone, etc.)
- Can push you (or back off) whenever appropriate
- Understands and respects your riding goals

The right kind of lesson

- Private: To practice specific skills, work on balance, gain confidence
- Semi-private: More personalized but also provides the opportunity to learn by watching other riders
- Group: More affordable and a great way to combine learning with a social experience

Developing a vocabulary

When you first start taking riding lessons, you might hear all kinds of things that make no sense to you. Things like:

- *Equal weight in both reins*
- *Soft elbows*
- *Following hands*
- *Leg on*

This is entirely normal, and even after you learn what certain terms and instructions mean, they still might not make sense in your body. Until you gain the muscle memory that connects the verbal instruction to the bodily action, ask your instructor to explain the action in more detail.

For example, if "heels down" makes no sense and feels like your ankles are strained and locked, think toes up instead. It's essentially the same action but with less strain in the middle of the foot.

Emergency dismount

Okay, so this isn't the most fun you'll ever have, but an emergency dismount can be a lifesaver, quite literally. While in most cases it's best to stick with a horse, even if they are running off, there are circumstances where an emergency dismount is the best option.

It's a bit more challenging in a Western saddle because of the horn, but the basic form is the same.

- Remove both feet from the stirrups.
- Place your hands on your horse's neck or over the saddle's horn

- Gain momentum by swinging both legs forward first, then swing your right leg back and over the saddle's cantle as you lean forward.
- Land with knees bent, facing forward.
- Try this at the halt, walk, and trot.

Bonus points: Teach your horse to stick around if you fall off.

After an emergency dismount in a controlled area, let go of the reins as you lay quickly down on the ground and simultaneously offer a treat. This helps your horse connect a person who has fallen off with a treat — a weird association, but one that might keep them by your side if you experience an "unplanned dismount."

Teach your horse to pick you up from a fence

Mounting with a mounting block is easy on an older rider's knees, but it's also better for your horse's back over their lifetime. But what happens when there's no block available?

You'll always have a place to mount if you teach your horse to pick you up at the fence (or off a log). The same cues can be taught to have them stand at the mounting block, too, and some people have even trained their horse to line up at the fence or mounting block when you call them from across the pasture.

There are three basic methods. Break each down into simple steps, and reward each part as your horse learns.

Method one

- They need to know how to respond to pressure at their poll first (from the halter).
- With your horse in a halter and a lead rope, move over to the fence and climb up to sit on the top rail.
- Start on your horse's near side (the usual side to mount from).

- Apply pressure by placing the lead rope into your left hand and pointing to the left. This is the direction they must go to line their body up for mounting.
- Don't add pressure if they are learning — wait for them to respond.
- Praise any steps forward, and give them scratches and pets in their itchy spots.
- Don't immediately swing your leg over when they line up. Let them rest and relax.
- You can climb off the fence, walk a circle, then ask again.
- Eventually, you'll put one leg over, with one leg still on the fence rail. Pause, let them relax, then remove the leg.
- Finally, mount up from the fence, tell them how great they are, and move off.
- Teach this from both sides.

Method two

- This method is used for picking up at the mounting block.
- You'll need a dressage whip or stick with a flag.
- Position your horse with their off side against the fence. You can also start in a corner, with the fence or a wall blocking forward motion, or with your horse facing a fence.
- With the dressage whip or stick, rhythmically tap their hip. You are aiming for annoyance, not pain. Add a verbal cue unique to this movement (i.e., a cluck or whistle).
- Keep tapping until their left hip shifts towards you or the back left foot moves. Stop and praise.
- Tap again, and wait for movement. Stop and praise.
- Eventually, they will swing their left hip all the way around. This is what you want. Aim towards softer cues until they respond to just the verbal cue.
- Once they have the idea at the fence, move to the mounting block.

- Position them so they can swing their left hip to line up with the block. This means they will face you just to the left of the mounting block.

Method three

- You'll need your horse in a halter and a dressage whip or stick without a flag or string.
- Lead your horse to the mounting block so they are facing you. You should position them so that you are visible in their left eye (so not exactly head-on).
- Holding the lead rope in your left hand, slowly bring the tip of the dressage whip up with your right.
- If they do not move towards it (and why would they?), reach to the other side of their body and tap their far hip until they shift their weight or step that left hip closer to you.
- Stop, praise, and tap again.
- Once they are up to the mounting block in the position you need for mounting, rest, praise, then walk away and start again.
- They may start to shift their hip when you lift the whip. Eventually, you might be able to lift your hand or a finger for them to settle themselves for mounting.

Troubleshooting

- If their hip swings away from the fence, send them in the other direction, and swing their hip back into place with a look.
- If they overshoot where you want them to be, soften the cue and release pressure faster.

- For method one, rhythmically bump the halter up until they make a change.
- At the fence, add a verbal cue, but be consistent with it.
- For method three, if they are too far away to reach the other side of their body with the whip, position them more diagonally so you can reach them (instead of with their nose perpendicular to the mounting block).

Go to a show

Even if your plans for your horse consist mainly of meandering trail rides and lazy hacks, going to a horse show is a great way to expose them to more potentially scary things: young children, announcements over loudspeakers, new horses. While you may not encounter a public address system in the woods, hanging out at a show builds a horse's trust and confidence in their person, which can eventually translate to all of their experiences with you. This is especially valuable for younger horses with limited experience.

Play games

Playing mounted games with your horse keeps things light while improving communication and connection. These aren't just for kids, either. Pay attention to how you cue your horse (and how they respond) to get lighter, faster responses as the games progress. The next three games are also great for meeting people at the barn.

- Red light, green light: A classic stop-and-go game
- Follow the leader: The leader sets the pace and direction
- Simon Says: Play this one mounted or on the ground

Have a ball

Large horse-proof balls can be very stimulating for your horse. They can be a good mental break for a horse bored with arena work (and a rider who wants a little fun in the saddle).

Start by desensitizing your horse to the ball on the ground, bouncing it from far away, rolling it around in front of you, and eventually bouncing it off your horse.

If even the presence of the ball is too much and sends your horse snorting and blowing across the arena, place it on the ground near you. Let it rest, and give your horse time to investigate on their own time. If they relax and begin to lower their head and lick or chew, that's enough. Move onto something else, then bring it out later or the next day.

Once they are comfortable with this strange new toy, encourage them to explore the ball and push it around the ring, either with their nose or legs and chest.

The best part about playing with a ball? It not only provides a fun and light-hearted way to play with your horse, but it also:

- Stretches your horse's back and lowers their head
- Piques your horse's curiosity
- Triggers a herding instinct
- Engages both eyes and feet

An exceptionally interested and engaged horse might begin to predict the ball's movement. If this occurs, it could be a good sign that your horse might enjoy cow work.

Mastery, connection, flow

Each of these contributes to your well-being, but the challenges of balancing a horse's needs with your own can be overwhelming, especially if you are locked into a regular routine that doesn't vary, is highly competitive, or places great mental demands on you. These mental demands can cause stress that your horse picks up on, with predictable results – a ride that is the opposite of a flowing, masterful connection.

As you approach each outing with your horse, focus on deep, even breathing that centers you directly in the moment that is happening, even if that's hoisting manure into a wheelbarrow. Shake off those creeping doubts or insecurities and return to the simple fact that being with your horse regularly is the best thing you can do for both of you.

Try a different discipline

This might be a one-off class or clinic, or you might take a break from your typical trail rides and ringwork to expand your equestrian horizons.

Some fun detours include:

- Mounted archery
- Pole bending
- Polo or polocross
- Driving
- Cross country
- Cow work (cutting, roping, etc.)

Go equicaching

Combine trail riding with navigation and give equicaching a try. This is an offshoot of geocaching, a scavenger hunt that utilizes GPS coordinates. Hundreds of thousands of caches (small boxes with little treats) are hidden around the world.

- For about $100, purchase a hand-held GPS (or use your phone if the service is reliable).
- Look for caches online, specifically in horse-friendly areas (use your zip code to find them).
- Ride to the cache, record your find, and take the little treat.
- It's traditional to leave a treat of your own (a small trinket).

Equicaching is best done with a buddy; most caches are not located right next to a trail and can require some searching. You may need someone to hold the horses while you search (plus, it's a good practice to trail ride with a buddy).

Set up a trail obstacle course

The International Mountain Trail Challenge Association (IMTCA) lists the following required trail obstacles in their handbook:

- Cross bucks: A series of logs with the ends propped up on larger logs and arranged so that they form cross rails
- Teeter totter: A wide platform that is balanced in the middle so that it moves as your horse crosses the center
- Balance beam: A narrow, stable beam that can be built like a raised bed or on a low platform
- 45 balance beam: A sturdy but narrow beam with a 45-degree bend that's wide enough for your horse to walk
- Turn box 42" (and 60"): A square box your horse climbs into, turns, and then climbs out of

- Raised logs: Set up like ground poles but slightly elevated
- Rock obstacle: Raised bed filled with different sizes of rocks
- Scramble: Randomly placed pile of different sizes of logs, sticks, and twigs
- Maze: Narrow course of logs that your horse navigates
- Logs: Actual large logs that your horse steps over
- Small bridge: A narrow bridge over shallow water

- Low back through: Logs or rails placed on the ground in a 90-degree angle you back your horse through
- Raised back through: Same as the Low Back Through but with rails at your horse's shoulder
- Water box: Rectangular shallow box of water your horse crosses (some people float a thin piece of wood with holes on the top for an added challenge)
- Cake box: Tiered platforms up to the center and down the other side
- Fan: Half circle of rails on the ground that your horse steps over
- Octagon box: A low octagonal obstacle filled with mud, water, or dirt

- Pinwheel: Spokes of logs set around a center to form a pinwheel (also sometimes referred to as a wagon wheel)
- Texas two-step: Two wide steps up to a platform and then down the other side
- Trench: Just what it sounds like, with high sides
- Gate: Opening and closing a gate

Some of these are easier to set up than others. If you are not yet confident in your riding partnership, you can start by leading your horse through obstacles before graduating to mounted work.

Go swimming

If you are lucky enough to keep your horse close to water, swimming can be a relaxing way to cool off in the hottest months.

Although some horses love water and will literally dive right in, don't assume that yours is comfortable in or around water. You may need to do some work before they are willing to dip a hoof in.

Start by letting them approach the water slowly. If they can't handle it head-on, approach in a zig-zag or serpentine instead. Allow them to approach and retreat — move them in a circle or half circle if you have space.

Reward even the smallest touch of hoof or nose to water and allow ample time for exploration and rest.

Teach your horse to pony (or pony another horse)

Ponying your horse off another horse is a great way to exercise two horses simultaneously. You'll need to be a confident rider with a balanced seat. The best way to learn how to pony another horse is to start with horses that are used to ponying and/or being ponied, but you'll still need strong, attentive riding skills to keep yourself and your horses organized.

Your riding horse needs to:

- Be calm and responsive to pressure on their poll
- Be willing to have another horse close to their body
- (Ideally) know verbal cues for "whoa"

Temperament matters, too. The ridden horse needs to be friendly, calm, and steady. They cannot be skittish or a bully. A rowdy youngster can be ponied effectively by a steady older horse that isn't spooky, but don't count on a spooky youngster as a lead horse!

The horse being ponied should be outfitted in a well-fitted halter. The lead rope to the ponied horse should have a couple of knots tied in it in case it slips out of your grasp. It should never be wrapped around the horn of the saddle.

Pony from both sides to keep your lead horse supple and balanced and to get practice for yourself.

Ponying should be practiced first in the ring. Start, stop, transition between gaits, back, turn, complete serpentines – then switch sides and do it all again. You can have a helper on the ground to move your ponied horse along if they need it. Use verbal cues (walk, trot, whoa, etc.) if necessary and useful.

Do not go faster than the ponied horse can handle on the trail. If your riding horse is sturdy and able to ride for hours but your ponied horse is a bit more fragile, base your distance on the ponied horse and stop when they are tired.

When riding, the ponied horse should be one head behind the riding horse, not dragging but not challenging the ridden horse either. There should be slack in the lead rope so they are not traveling forward with a bend in their neck.

In terms of holding the ponying rope and the reins, if the ponied horse is experienced and calm, you can treat the ponying lead rope as part of the reins. Otherwise, hold the lead rope separately. Do not ever wrap it around your hand or saddle horn, and don't try to hold a horse who is pulling back or fighting hard. Let them go, dismount, and then go get them.

Know your limits. If you are attempting to pony a horse and do not feel confident in the ponied horse or your mount, do not ride out. Practice more in the ring, then come back to it.

Go overnight camping

Maybe you've dreamed of roughing it in the woods with your horse, sipping morning coffee surrounded by nature while your horse munches a contented breakfast before mounting up and climbing into the hills. Instead of heading directly to the backcountry, inexperienced campers might want to consider camping at an established horse campsite. These often have stalls or round pens for horses, plus marked trails and bathhouses for campers.

Of course, backcountry camping offers a solitary experience through genuinely wild landscapes. If you have learned to pony a horse, longer camping trips are possible, too. A ponied packhorse means you can head into the backcountry for days or weeks at a time (depending on your experience and stamina for roughing it). If this sounds good to you, you'll need to:

- Learn how to pack a horse properly
- Consider the feed and forage needs of your horse(s)
- Acquire camping gear
- Plan meals
- Assemble safety gear and a first-aid kit
- Plan a route (consider water along the route)

You might also want to locate a trail outfitter to see if they offer navigation, safety, and trip-planning courses. It can be beneficial to learn how to pack a horse in person, as can taking a short overnight trip to see how things go before heading out for a week on your own.

Hobbling and using a highline

Taking a containment system on a backcountry trip may not be possible, and even the most connected horse might wander off. So how do you keep your horse safe and close by with the freedom to move on their own, roll, and graze?

Teach your horse to hobble tie or tie to a highline. You'll use each technique at different times. For example, hobbling is a good option when no sturdy trees are available, and a highline works for young or inexperienced horses who need to move more.

Hobbles can be affixed to two or three legs. The material should be soft but sturdy and fitted securely around your horse's pastern.

Highlines run above your horse's head and attach to trees. The horse is clipped onto the highline with enough rope so that they can move freely (and sometimes graze and lie down).

Whichever you choose, train your horse at home before you try it on the trail.

PART III

KEEPING YOUR HORSE HEALTHY

"Horses were never wrong. They always did what they did for a reason, and it was up to you to figure it out." Jeannette Walls

She was at the far end of the pasture and moving away from me. The rope halter hung loose in my hand, and my approach was casual, but Lark had my number. She cast a side eye at me every time I got closer, then picked up her feet and trotted away, ears pinned back.

This is what you get when you adopt a rescue horse from a kill pen, I thought as I tried to figure out the best approach. Who knows what traumas they have suffered? How can they possibly learn to trust another human?

I was eventually able to catch and halter Lark. Once she was haltered, my plans changed, and we stayed in the pasture that day, walking from one spot of delicious grass to another before I let her go and sat down to hang out with the herd for a while.

This frustrating day turned out to be one of the most critical junctures in our relationship, though. Restoring Lark's mental and physical health became a holistic learning experience. I needed to figure out why she was running away before we could progress in our relationship (and training). A bodywork appointment identified pain points across her body. A re-evaluation of her diet indicated a need for fewer concentrates and more high-quality forage. We moved back to the ground and started slowly, rebuilding trust and preparing her to continue her journey with a professional trainer and, eventually, a home where she would be a sweet and loving pasture ornament.

Lark came to me advertised as a safe riding horse, but only through attention to the horse that actually stepped off the trailer was it possible to see that she was crying for rest and peace. Focusing on the horse in front of you can lead to a bonded partnership unlike any other, and it's always a good time to strengthen your relationship with your horse.

For many horses, it's just not possible to dive into groundwork and riding. They have been scarred by careless or intentional abuse or misuse. They show their aversion to humans by running away in the pasture, rearing, biting, shutting down, and exhibiting other learned, self-protective behaviors.

There is also new research indicating that many equestrians (experienced and novice) underestimate pain's role in how horses behave. From ulcers or weight fluctuations brought on by stress, diet, or metabolic issues to tight areas of the body from past injuries and ill-fitting tack, horses tell us when they are in pain and hope desperately that we are listening. This pain may be a result of a specific injury, changes due to age, or an accumulation of daily stress that adds up to an overall sore, tight body that just doesn't feel good when carrying a rider.

In addition to physical ailments, your horse may be unfit or incapable of what you're asking them to do. Horses that have been out of work for a period of time are just like humans when they begin to exercise again — they need gradually increasing amounts of work to strengthen their bodies (and to bring their minds along, too).

This section on keeping your horse healthy starts with exercise; the different stretches and activities can be modified up or down to suit your horse's level of fitness. These are mostly done on the ground, with a section on using trot poles to develop better fitness in your horse under saddle.

The next chapter, grooming, is about more than just presenting a beautifully turned out horse. Grooming mimics herd behavior in many ways. Most horses find it relaxing and enjoyable, but it's also a good way to get to know your horse and their health better. If something is off, you'll see it sooner.

This section, and this book, ends with bodywork for connection. The study of equine bodywork is the work of a lifetime, but there are many things you can start in the comfort of your own barn. When you lay your hands on your horse, magical things can happen — for both of you.

CHAPTER 10

STRETCHING, LONG WALKS, AND EXERCISE

"The essential joy of being with horses is that it brings us in contact with the rare elements of grace, beauty, spirit, and freedom." Sharon Ralls Lemon

You may have entered horse ownership with vivid images of long rides through the woods or blue ribbons fluttering from your horse's bridle. But what happens when you don't have time for a long ride, your horse is injured and resting, or you want to bond more before you hop aboard?

And if your horse is injured or older, is there any way you can help them be more comfortable and heal? These exercises are great for horses on layup and riders who need a break but want to maintain their horse's fitness and flexibility.

Keep in mind:

- Any stretching should be done carefully and with respect to the horse's flexibility, health, and ability.
- Go slowly and pay attention to your horse's response.
- Licking, chewing, and yawning are positive signs of relaxation and release.
- Stretches can be done before and after riding (or on their own).

Carrot stretches

Carrot stretches are named for the crunchy orange vegetable some equestrians use to motivate their horses to stretch their body. You can substitute sugar-free treats or use clicker training if your horse is on a specialized diet.

Carrot stretch to the side

This stretch is like a lateral crunch for your horse. The benefits include:

1. An increase in lateral flexibility
2. More suppleness through the body
3. More stability in the core

You are encouraging your horse to reach to the side and down. To do that:

- Stand next to your horse where you would attach the girth/cinch.
- Get their attention with a treat and encourage them to bend their head and neck laterally to reach for it.
- As they reach, lower the carrot to just below their knee.
- Let the carrot graze their lips.
- Hold the stretch for three to five seconds before you give them the carrot.
- For older horses, you may only get a second or two of the stretch at first.
- Repeat up to three times per session on both sides.

As flexibility increases, stand closer to the horse's tail. You can also add to the stretch by holding the end of their tail as they reach, but don't jump into this movement until they have gained sufficient flexibility.

Practice in a smaller space if your horse steps backward to get the treat or turns their whole body, and allow your horse to straighten their neck between stretches.

Carrot stretch between the legs

This deeply stretches the muscles along the withers, neck, and back. It's equivalent to a human sit-up and helps horses to:

1. Build core stability and strength
2. Increase muscles along the back
3. Have better posture in general
4. Lift and engage the muscles in the belly to support movement

This can be very challenging for older horses, so if you have a senior equine partner don't ask them to stretch too deeply initially.

If your horse can reach the ground to graze, chances are they can do this more structured stretch for a treat. Make sure your horse is comfortable with things in the blind spot underneath their chin before you start this stretch.

- Stand close to their shoulder and present the carrot, bringing it down to the ground and close to their front legs.
- Keep it close to their lips and hold the stretch for a few seconds before letting them take it.
- Some horses bend a front leg to make the stretch easier. This is okay, but only if they are lifting their belly and engaging their back muscles, too. If they continue to bend their leg to reach, back off until they gain more flexibility.

Carrot chin to chest

Some horses lose flexibility in the poll as they age (or if they have been sitting for a while). This can make collection hard, throwing your horse off balance when you ride.

A carrot chin to chest is a simple stretch that can help loosen and relax a tense poll.

- Stand just at the base of their neck.
- Introduce the carrot to the horse just below their mouth.
- Bring the carrot to their chest, and hold it just out of reach for a few seconds.
- Some horses will only be able to hold this briefly.
- Repeat three to five times.
- Allow them to lift their head between stretches.

Carrot chin to knee

- Use the same method as the carrot chin to chest, instead guiding your horse to touch their knee. This is a good intermediate stretch if your horse struggles with chin to chest or a stretch between their legs.

Passive osteopathic stretches

Unlike carrot stretches where you ask your horse to actively reach for a treat to stretch their body, passive stretches only require them to relax and lean into the stretch. These stretches:

1. Increase flexibility
2. Promote joint health
3. Maintain (and improve) range of motion
4. Release tension in the fascia
5. Help improve body awareness and posture

While some believe these should only be done on a horse after they are warmed up, others promote this type of stretching to ease a horse into exercise. Regardless of when you do them, there are a few general guidelines.

- Move slowly. Don't ask for too much, too soon, especially on cold ligaments.
- Make sure your horse feels safe and relaxed before stretching.
- Hold each stretch for a few seconds. This encourages your horse to lean into the stretch.
- Look for signs of relaxation and release.

Shoulder stretch

This stretch loosens up tight shoulders and releases muscle tension.

- Pick up a front leg as if you were going to pick the hoof.
- Turn to face your horse, supporting underneath the knee and the pastern.
- Brace yourself by bending your knees slightly.
- Press the leg up toward to body, keeping the knee and pastern level and focusing on lifting into the shoulder (not raising the hoof).
- Repeat three to five times.
- You can also hold the leg for a few seconds, waiting to see if your horse will

drop into the leg to stretch the shoulder on their own.

- Release and repeat on the other side.

Front leg stretch

This lengthens your horse's triceps and back muscles. It's also a great stretch to perform after saddling up to ensure no skin is pinched beneath the cinch/girth.

- Pick up the front foot as usual.
- Gradually stretch the foot straight forward, supporting the foot and pastern.
- Hold for ten seconds or so, then release slowly (don't just drop the foot).
- Repeat once more, then move to the other foot.
- If your horse snatches their foot, they are either not used to this, or you've gone too far.
- If your horse steps forward as you stretch, release sooner so they understand you're asking them to stretch, not step forward.

Back leg stretch to the front

- Perform the same type of stretch on each back leg, supporting the flexor tendon and the pastern.
- Extend the back leg straight toward the front leg — not out to the side.
- This is also called hind limb protraction, and it stretches the large hamstring muscles.

Back leg stretch to the back

- Cue your horse to pick up their hind leg as if you are going to pick up their hoof.
- Support the lower leg and fetlock as you stretch the leg straight behind and angled down from the hindquarters.

- They may keep their leg bent for a few moments. Give the horse time to relax and release into the stretch.
- Hold the stretch for 10-15 seconds, then slowly guide the tip of the hoof to the ground. Let them rest with that leg extended briefly before moving to the other side.
- Repeat this at least once more on each leg.

Spine stretch

- Place one hand on their withers.
- Place the other hand on the point of the hip.
- Press the hand on the hip point gently back as if you were stretching the horse's side like putty.
- Hold the stretch for 10 to 20 seconds.
- If you notice the back muscles twitching, stay where you are and let them gradually release.
- If the twitching worsens, it may indicate discomfort. Slowly release the stretch.
- If your horse moves away from the pressure, make sure you are pressing back toward their tail, not the center of their body.
- Movement may also mean discomfort, so pay attention.

Belly lifts

- Use belly lifts to help build muscle along the topline.
- With claw-like fingers (or a stiff rubber curry), gently rub under your horse's belly from where the girth sits to about a hand's width in front of your horse's sheath or teats.
- They should lift their back muscles and slightly tuck their hind in response.
- Some horses are very sensitive under their bellies. Take care and watch for signs

of annoyance (i.e., tail swishing and pinned ears).

- Repeat three to five times on both sides.

Back lifts (a.k.a. the butt tuck)

- Make sure your horse is safe with a person behind them before performing this.
- Find the crease in your horse's hindquarters. It's somewhere between the outside of their hip and the tail.
- Run your fingertips down this crease, "tickling" them to encourage them to tuck their pelvis and lift their back.
- Maintain the tuck as long as possible, but pay attention to signs they might kick out.

Tension release in the jaw

Horses hold a lot of tension in their mouth and jaw. This causes bracing that runs through their body. Myofascial release is an easy way to help your horse relax.

- Place the web of skin between your thumb and forefinger on your horse's gums underneath their upper lip.
- Don't move, squeeze, or press. Just let your hand make contact.
- Your horse may start to open their mouth, flop their tongue around, or make chewing motions. This is your horse leaning into the release.
- Let your horse flap their gums around as long as they want to. If they move their head up or down, maintain contact without adding pressure. This is just them releasing tension in the way they need to.
- When they're done, your horse will use their upper lip to flick your hand away.

Take long walks

Taking a long walk with your horse is relaxing and a great way to bond. You aren't asking them to carry the burden of your shifting weight. You aren't expecting any type of work or schooling.

All you are doing is experiencing a little nature therapy with your equine friend.

Long walks are a great way to get some gentle exercise, but they can also be used to:

- Introduce your horse to an unfamiliar trail
- Practice better leading
- Hike a difficult trail for better fitness (for both of you!)

It's also a different way to experience what your horse sees from their perspective. It's easy to forget that a horse's view is different than ours when we are mounted. Down on the ground, we can better feel the instability of the trail, see the movement of the trees and foliage, and hear what's coming up on the trail. This unique perspective makes you a more empathetic rider.

Walking or hiking with your horse also more closely mimics herd behavior. Horses spend hours every day walking from place to place together. This is a good opportunity to watch and learn their body language as they navigate the trail without a saddle or rider.

If you are a nervous or anxious rider, walking a trail first can give you more confidence, too. It's hard to convince your horse you're a confident leader if you're nervous about falling off. Walking helps you face unfamiliar territory until you feel in control of your own emotions.

Finally, walking or hiking with your horse is an excellent way to build strength and muscle in both horse and human. See if you can incorporate some hills into your stroll for the best results.

Exercise and the senior horse

Some riders are inclined to use their horse less as they age. While it's always good to pay attention to changes in a horse's changing abilities, movement is critical for healthy senior equines. As with people, "motion is lotion." Standing at the round bale all day or in a stall contributes to a faster decline in aging horses. Movement keeps joints lubricated and healthy.

Exercise on varied terrain is also essential for stalled horses of any age who do not have unlimited turnout. Taking a walk regularly adds to your horse's long and healthy life.

Exercising on a lunge line: poles edition

When you exercise your horse on a lunge line, you can better see how they move when they're feeling good. Once you are familiar with your horse and all of their quirks, this can help you spot more subtle signs of lameness.

Additionally, it's easier for your horse to learn how to balance and better use their body when they don't have to support the sometimes-unbalanced weight of a rider. These exercises, completed a few times a week for a couple of minutes at a time, help to strengthen your horse before they have to carry a rider.

A few general guidelines:

- You are not aiming for exhaustion in your horse, just a brief workout and muscle activation.
- If you get dizzy as you lunge, make sure you walk in a circle, not just spin around.
- Your horse should be familiar with lunging before adding these exercises.

- Poles are usually set about two and a half feet apart, but you may have to adjust for your horse's stride length.
- Complete these exercises three times a week (or as needed once fitness improves).

Building the core

A strong core means a healthy back. The core muscles may be underdeveloped and rarely utilized for horses accustomed to traveling around hollow, with very little propulsion from behind. This is a great simple exercise to get them using their core.

The setup:

- Five poles total, spaced two and a half feet apart
- First two poles flat on the ground
- Next two poles with one alternating end raised
- Final pole is raised on both ends (just under a foot off the ground)

The action:

- Send your horse at an active walk through the poles five to seven times in each direction.
- They should stretch down and through their back as they lift their feet to accommodate the uneven heights.
- Some stumbling and confusion is normal at first. Give them time to adjust their movement.

Weak side strength building

Just as people are stronger and more agile with one hand, most horses have one side that is stronger. This exercise helps bring more strength to the weak side. You can also use this exercise to develop a better canter lead.

The setup:

- Create a lane with trot poles running parallel. This encourages straightness.
- Set up four poles about two and a half feet apart, each with one side raised.

The action:

- Warm your horse up at the walk first.
- When your horse is ready and attentive, send them through the center of the poles with their weaker side closest to the raised ends of the poles.
- For developing a canter lead, put the opposite side of the lead that is hardest next to the raised end (e.g., for challenges on the left lead, the raised end of the pole should be on your horse's right side).
- Go through the poles at a trot up to ten times on the weaker side, then send your horse through on their strong side up to five times.

Balancing circle

This utilizes trot poles at different angles on one side of the circle and a group of ground poles on the opposite side to engage the quads and develop more stability.

The setup:

- Four ground poles set up on one side
- Four poles set on the opposite side of the circle the same distance apart but with one end of each raised
- The raised end should alternate (the left end of the first is raised, the right end of the second is raised, and so on)

The action:

- Send your horse in a circle through both sets of poles at a forward walk.
- There should be one step between each pole,
- If your horse struggles to maintain a forward walk or is adding a step between poles, move the poles closer to each other.

- Repeat the circle seven times both ways. Trot as your horse gets more fit.

Riding trot poles

Adding trot poles (a.k.a., cavaletti when they are slightly raised and ground poles when they are not) to a workout encourages a horse to lift their feet and properly use their body.

- Start with two poles nine feet apart. This should produce three walk steps, two trot steps, and one canter stride.
- For more exercise at the walk, set up three poles three feet apart.
- At the trot, two poles at four and a half feet.
- Enter and exit each pole at its center, and make sure to approach in both directions.
- Trot poles are also a great introduction to trail obstacles and jumping.
- For a more advanced setup that helps create a bend in your horse's body, place four poles at the cardinal directions of a circle (it will resemble a compass).
- Ride the poles while maintaining a bend in your horse's body.
- Use seat cues rather than relying on your reins: point your hips in the direction you'd like to go while keeping the inside leg on and the outside rein firm against their neck.
- Start at the walk, then move to the trot.
- Notice where your horse's shoulder moves in or out of the circle, and adjust your pressure. For example, if your horse's shoulder bulges out and they start to move out of the circle, firm up your outside rein and leg and open the inside rein a bit.

STANLEY
BRAID-ETTES
PITCHER PARTNERS

CHAPTER 11

GROOMING

"Don't be the rider who gallops all night and never sees the horse beneath him." *Rumi*

A beautifully turned-out horse is a joy to watch and a pleasure to ride. More importantly, regular, careful grooming keeps your horse's skin and coat healthy and can alert you to any minor scrapes, punctures, or other injuries they may have sustained in the pasture.

Grooming is also a time for bonding. Your horse may turn around and nibble on your back as you brush their shoulder or withers. This mimics the mutual grooming that happens in the pasture and indicates that your horse is relaxed, happy, and enjoying the attention.

A basic grooming kit should include the following items:

- Hoof pick (with or without the stiff brush on the end)
- Rubber curry comb
- Stiff-bristled body brush
- Soft body brush
- Hairbrush or wide-toothed comb (for mane and tail)
- Shedding blade or block
- Soft rag

You can, of course, add items as you need them, including:

- Clippers

- Horse shampoo
- Coat conditioner
- Leave-in conditioner (for braiding)
- Whitener
- Hoof oil
- Pulling comb
- Hair bows or elastics for braiding
- Scissors
- Sweat scraper

Daily exam

Carefully look over your horse for scratches and dings they have picked up when playing in the fields with their friends. Most minor scratches do not require medical attention, but a minor-seeming scratch can turn into an infection. Sometimes something that looks like a minor scratch may actually be a puncture (a potentially more serious injury).

Examining your horse daily helps you to know when something is amiss and makes it easier to act quickly if necessary.

This daily once-over also uncovers any skin issues. Rain rot is a type of skin infection (also called rain scald). It causes itchy, sometimes painful scabs and can become serious if left untreated.

Checking your horse daily catches minor issues before they require more serious intervention. Keep in mind that if you do find rain rot or other skin issues, you'll need to:

- Wash and disinfect your brushes
- Avoid sharing brushes in the barn
- Treat the infection

Leg check

Run your hands down all four of your horse's legs regularly to check for swelling and heat (which could indicate an injury).

It can be difficult at first to figure out what you are feeling for but keep at it. The more familiar you are with your horse's legs when they are healthy, the better you are able to recognize quickly when they are off. This could be the difference between a minor bump that needs cold-hosing and rest and a significant injury that requires surgery or months of rehabilitation.

The daily leg check is also a great time to check for bot eggs. Bot eggs are laid by flies that land on a horse's legs. When horses use their teeth to itch their legs, they ingest the eggs, which hatch into parasitic worms. These eggs are small, white or pale yellow, and difficult to remove by brushing alone.

Clean bot eggs off (generally in spring and fall) using a bot knife with a short, curved blade or a grooming block (used more commonly for shedding out a horse in the spring).

Pick feet

Your horse's feet should be picked out daily, with a visual inspection for:

- Thrush: An infection in the frog characterized by a foul-smelling black substance
- Stones: Lodged in the frog or hoof
- Cracks: In the hoof wall
- Signs of abscess: In the bottom of the foot, the coronary band, or the heel bulbs

---

Learn to rasp between trims

Trimming your horse, or at least rasping between trims, is a money-saving tip that also helps you learn more about your horse's anatomy and how their body works. This can help you be more aware when something is off.

The best way to do this is to read as much as possible about trimming and rasping and work with a farrier you trust. Sometimes a farrier will give your horse a "set up" trim that you can work to maintain and have checked occasionally (feedback is always good!).

It is a misconception that a horse must be shod. Research indicates a "bare" foot is as healthy even for horses in regular work, but it's important to have a professional thoroughly evaluate your horse's feet before making any changes.

The bonus? Knowing more about the mechanics of your horse's hooves makes you a more informed horse owner, even if you don't choose to trim on your own.

Spray clean feet with ACV

Apple cider vinegar is a natural antibacterial treatment. Spraying watered-down ACV on feet after a thorough cleaning helps to keep thrush and other bacteria at bay. Add a few drops of tea tree oil to your spray for more protection.

Treat thrush

There are several thrush treatments on the market. While the best treatment is prevention, if your horse has thrush:

- Keep the feet as dry as possible.
- Treat with ThrushBuster, Gold Bond medicated powder, ACV, tea tree oil, or sugardine (see sidebar).
- Monitor and call your vet if the thrush does not improve.

Create sugardine for thrush

Sugardine is a paste of sugar and povidone-iodine that, when applied to thrushy areas, is an effective and affordable remedy for thrush.

Mix white table sugar with enough povidone-iodine to form a thick paste. Press the paste down into the sides of the frog. Repeat as necessary, and mix up a fresh batch when needed.

Take pictures of hooves

A horse's hooves are essential to their overall health and well-being. Pictures help you keep track of a hoof's changes over time.

- Pictures should be taken from both sides, the front, the full body, and behind.
- The camera should be level to the ground (which should itself be level and free of debris for the best pictures).
- Take pictures of the bottom of the foot, straight down from the heel bulbs, to show the height of each heel.
- Cracks and slopes may mean a hoof needs to be trimmed more frequently.
- Horizontal bands can indicate stress, dietary changes, or a mild laminitic event.
- Pictures can also show if a hoof has flares or is unbalanced.
- These pictures are invaluable tools, especially if you decide to learn to trim your own horse's feet.

Clean hoof-trimming tools

If you do decide to trim your horse, you must keep your tools clean and ready. Your hoof knives should be sharp. Soak your rasp in WD-40 a few times a year and clean it with a wire brush after each use.

Clean body, healthy horse

A basic daily grooming proceeds in a specific order. Take your time with each step.

Start with a curry

Currying your horse daily is the best way to keep them clean without removing the natural protective oils in their coat. Currying stimulates blood flow and loosens scurf, the flakey dry skin and dirt that accumulates at the base of a horse's haircoat. Use a firm but not harsh counter-clockwise circular motion all over. Currying directly after a workout when pores are open allows for even more dirt removal.

Thoroughly curry your horse, from nose to tail and ears to hooves. Be careful around sensitive areas, like the belly and the legs. Use a hand-shaped, fine-nubbed curry glove to rub down each leg.

Alternatively, you can sit on your horse with a curry and work on their hindquarters/withers/topline. On tall horses, these areas can be neglected. A good rub loosens dirt, stimulates blood flow, and generally feels really good to your horse.

Be aware of any sensitive areas as you rub. If the horse flinches from contact, back off a bit and be more gentle.

Follow with a stiff brush

Once you've massaged the dirt and grime to the surface, use a stiff-bristled brush and a quick flick of the wrist to remove it.

Finish with shine

A soft brush after the stiff one removes any final dirt and redistributes the oils you've raised all along the hair shaft. This last step makes your horse shiny and soft.

You can also use a very small, soft brush to gently remove dirt from your horse's face. Be gentle — some horses are very sensitive to this.

Give your horse a bath

This should only be done in warm weather, both for your comfort and your horse's comfort. Show barns may bathe their horses year-round, and sometimes a bath is necessary when skin issues or injuries occur in cold weather, but warm-weather baths are best.

Be certain that your horse is desensitized to water before you begin. If your horse is nervous or uncomfortable, you may want to put the actual bathing off to train them to accept water.

- Before the bath itself, curry your horse to loosen dead skin.
- Give your horse a brush with a stiff brush to remove any shedding hair or dirt you bring up.
- Fill a bucket of water and add soap. Tea tree soap is great for this – antibacterial and natural - but you can also use a specifically formulated horse shampoo.
- Soak a large sponge, and, working from the neck and moving back to the rump and down the legs, wash your horse.
- You can add more shampoo to the mane and tail for a deep cleaning. These also benefit from a leave-in conditioner after the rinse.
- The most important part of the wash is the rinse – be certain you have rinsed your horse thoroughly to prevent irritation.
- If you want your horse's coat to shine after rinsing, dilute a cup of apple cider vinegar in a bucket of water and rinse your horse with this after rinsing out the soap.
- Finish the bath by wiping off your horse's face and cleaning their ears and nostrils.
- On hot days, use a sweat scraper to remove excess water, then take the opportunity to hand graze your horse while they dry.

Clean your horse's sheath (geldings and stallions)

For this job, you will need a horse that is used to hands in and around their sheath. This is a not the most pleasant job, but it's important for your horse's comfort and health.

- You will need sheath cleaner, paper towels, warm water, and gloves.
- Put a dollop of sheath cleaner on your hand and reach into your horse's sheath, massaging to release the dirt.
- Clean all the way up the sheath, rinsing thoroughly to remove the sheath cleaner.
- The last step in sheath cleaning is to reach into the folded skin to find the "bean," a whitish ball of smegma that needs to be removed.
- If you do not remove this ball, it can grow to the size of a walnut, obstructing urine and causing serious health problems.
- Be mindful of your horse's feet and sensitive to any discomfort they may feel as you clean.
- They may lift their back hoof to swat at their belly if they are nervous or uncomfortable.
- Take care to rinse all of the sheath cleaner, as dried soap can be itchy and uncomfortable.

Clean your horse's sheath twice a year. If you hear a squeaking noise as you trot around the ring and it has been a while since your horse's sheath was cleaned, that's a good time to get started.

Clean your horse's udder (mares)

The area between a mare's teats accumulates a black, pasty substance that can be itchy and uncomfortable. As with the sheath, make sure your horse is desensitized to hands on and around the udder before attempting this.

- Check a mare's udder at least once weekly, especially in warm weather.
- Use either a baby wipe or a cloth with damp water to remove all of the substance.
- Soap is not necessary, but when you give your horse a bath you can use horse shampoo, making sure to rinse thoroughly.

Remove chestnuts/ergots

Chestnuts and ergots are the odd, sometimes hard growths on the inside of a horse's knees on the front and hind legs. They fall off of their own accord, but they are soft enough to remove after a bath or on a lazy day when you hang out with your horse in the pasture, being sociable and scratching itchy places.

Cowboy legend says that if you put a chestnut in your pocket, all the horses in the field will follow you.

Grooming the mane and tail

Braid tail

There are many different ways to braid a horse's tail. A simple braid is best for the pasture. A French braid looks fancy and tidy in the show ring.

Whatever braid you choose, always start with a clean, dry, detangled tail. To prevent breakage, spray with a leave-in conditioner to make combing through the tail easier. Finish your braid with styling gel to smooth flyaway hair for a more polished look.

Clip a bridle path

The bridle path is the area behind the ears where the bridle's headpiece rests (also found on a Western headstall and still useful if you use a Western headstall without a headpiece). A clean bridle path makes it easy to bridle and keeps a horse looking neat (no hair to rub or get stuck).

- Desensitize your horse to scissors and clippers around their ears if needed.
- To determine how long to make the bridle path, gently bend one ear back (to the side, not straight backward). The bridle path should be trimmed to where the tip of the ear touches.
- If this seems like a lot of mane to trim, trim just an inch wider than your bridle's headpiece.
- If you have never trimmed the bridle path, it is best to cut the hair with scissors and then neaten it with clippers.

Roach Mane

Roaching is the process of completely shaving off your horse's mane.

Why on earth would you do that, you ask?

- Some horses grow a naturally skimpy mane.
- Some horses rub huge chunks of their mane off on a tree or fence.
- Some horses get their mane chewed off during mutual grooming.

If you are headed to a show and your horse meets you at the barn with a half-chewed mane, roaching is generally the only option you have to make your horse look nice.

Some horse owners prefer the roached look to show off a particularly pretty or strong neck (Fjords and certain draft breeds are known for roached manes). Some owners don't want to fuss with a mane.

To roach:

- Cut long hair first.
- Finish with clippers.
- Keep the forelock.

Bang the tail

Banging the tail is cutting the tail to make the ends even. Many jumper and dressage horses have banged tails, and some owners like to bang especially long tails to keep them from the muddy ground in the winter.

- Start with a clean, brushed tail and sharp scissors.
- Slide your hand under the tail to imitate how the horse naturally carries its tail when in action.
- Gather the hair at the end of the tail into a tight bunch.
- Cut straight across, being careful not to pull additional stray hairs downward.

Your final result should be a clean, straight edge across the base of the tail. Banged tails generally rest above the ankle; any higher tends to look strange. Some horse owners will cut off several inches more to above the hocks and use the hair for bracelets and fly switches.

Put up the tail

Putting up a horse's tail is generally reserved for winter, well after fly season, in areas where mud, snow, and ice make a horse's tail a nightmare to keep tidy.

Many draft breeds have their tails put up permanently as part of their regular grooming. This keeps manure out of the tail when a horse is working and shows off their powerful hindquarters.

Others who regularly put up tails for the winter swear that it adds up to six inches to their horse's tails every year when they unwrap it.

- Thoroughly brush and condition your horse's tail.
- Braid the tail in a simple braid, starting approximately two inches below the bottom of the tailbone.
- Braid to the bottom of the tail and tie with an elastic band.
- Take the end of the tail and loop up through the top of the braid (if your horse has a long tail, you may need to do this twice).
- Using vet wrap (use only white vet wrap on a light-colored tail; other colored wraps may stain), poke the end of the wrap through the top of the braid (under the tailbone) and wrap the braid vertically.
- Then wrap the braid horizontally, many times, squeezing the braid into a compact column as you do (the braid will start off lumpy and fat and end as a slimmer column of vet wrap-covered braid).
- As you wrap, pay attention to the top of the braid, as that is where the wrap usually begins to fray first, but always remember to leave plenty of room between the braid and the tailbone. The braid should swing freely from below the tailbone.
- Finish the job by cutting the vet wrap and squeezing tightly one last time to seal all the layers together.

Wraps should last two to three weeks in winter if done correctly. Replace when the wrap becomes frayed or torn.

You can also put up a tail in the summer. When you finish, add 20 lengths of baling twine to the final wrap so your horse has a swish for flies.

Pull/thin the mane

A pulled mane is a well-groomed look for the show ring and is easy to maintain on the trail.

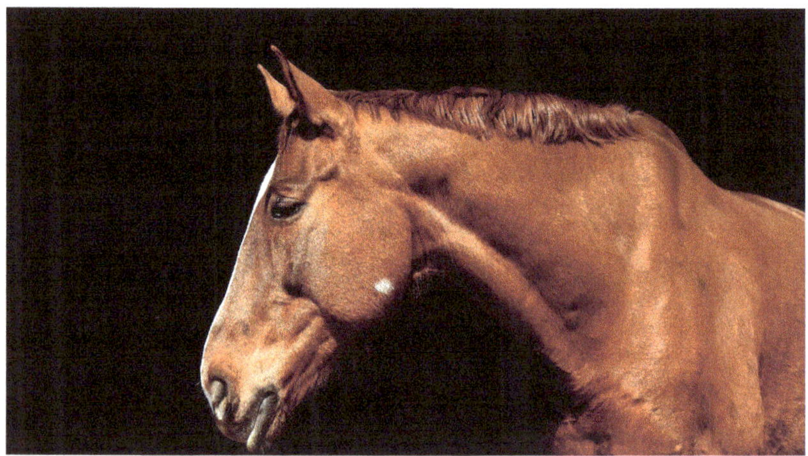

You need a comb and a clean (but not oiled), tangle-free mane. Hair comes out best when the pores are open and relaxed, so pulling a mane after exercise may make the job easier.

- Start at either the ears or the withers.
- Take a section of mane (2-3") and slide your hand down until you only have the longest hairs left (only about 5-10 strands at a time).
- Back comb the short hairs until you are only holding the longer hairs.
- Pull down quickly and with one sharp tug, and you should have the long hair out.
- If the hair does not come out or your horse seems uncomfortable, start with fewer hairs.

- You can also do a small section of mane at a time.

Your goal is a tidy mane, not an unpleasant battle. If you are starting with a long mane, the whole process could take a week or two of small, daily pulling, but after that, you should be able to keep up with it more easily.

Band the mane

Banding the mane is used most often in Western disciplines. Banding is simply applying elastics to the base of the mane by the neck.

- As always, start with a clean, tangle-free mane.
- Apply elastics to the base of the mane in even intervals.
- You can apply a "training spray" (watered-down hair gel works or purchase spray formulated especially for equines) to make the mane lie flat.
- It is important to know that the shorter the mane, the higher the possibility of it sticking up or out.
- For a mane to lay flat, banding works best on manes that are four inches or longer.

CHAPTER 12

BODYWORK FOR CONNECTION

"With the knowledge that kindness doesn't automatically mean loss of watchfulness, judgment or control, we realize that we can allow ourselves the great pleasure of befriending our horses." Linda Tellington-Jones

One of the sweetest ways to bond with your horse is to offer them bodywork. This is a form of care that helps them release tension in their bodies to better relax their mind. Just as a long massage helps humans de-stress, so, too, does bodywork for horses.

No matter which type of bodywork you experiment with, there are a few guidelines.

Pay attention to your horse

Being present is one of the best things you can do while practicing any bodywork techniques on your horse. They can feel your distraction, your haste, your desire to get onto the next thing. It's better for both of you to have short, focused, and totally involved sessions instead of longer, distracted, rushed interactions.

Keeping sessions short and light also allows you to better gauge how they react and what they want more of. If your horse has never had bodywork, it can also be difficult for them to relax in an unfamiliar situation.

Tailor what you're doing to their response

They may start out uncertain if the technique is new — look for signs of relaxation (i.e., lowered head, licking and chewing, softening of tension in the muzzle).

Use the appropriate level of touch

Your goal is not to annoy or tickle your horse, but you also don't want to cause pain. Again, looking for signs like ear pinning, tightness in the hind end, and other indications of pain or annoyance help you to adjust your pressure appropriately.

Work with a buddy

If you are uncomfortable treating your horse in the pasture or tied in the barn, ask a friend to hold the lead rope while you work. They can report any responses and offer a level of safety and comfort for you, too.

Learn more

If your horse responds to a specific type of bodywork, dig deeper. Clinics in your area, online tutorials and videos, and equine bodywork manuals can all take you deeper into the anatomy and physiology of your equine friend. They also offer a more detailed explanation of many different bodywork techniques.

Acupressure

Acupressure is a type of traditional Chinese medicine (TCM). TCM identifies 365 points along 12 different meridians in the body. Each meridian is linked to an organ system or system. Clear meridians allow qi (pronounced "chee") to flow throughout the body, bringing balance and harmony to physical and emotional health.

But each of these points can become blocked or sluggish. If they are blocked or slowed, pain, tension, and agitation can result. Instead of the thin needles used in acupuncture, acupressure applies pressure to specific points on the body to release blockages and restore the flow of qi. Many horses find a session of acupressure deeply relaxing.

As with people, different horses have personalities that benefit from different types of acupressure. Horses might prefer one of three techniques.

1. Balancing: A harmonizing technique that is applied for one minute
2. Yin: Soothing pressure applied more firmly for two minutes
3. Yang: Stimulation that is feather-light and lasts just 30 seconds

Although a professional bodyworker can better assess and prescribe specific treatment for your horse, many horses benefit from applying acupressure to just three areas of the body: the shen men (Spirit's gate), nei guan (inner gate), and bai hui (heaven's gate).

It's easy to get started on your own. Prepare by focusing your attention first. Before you begin:

- Center yourself by breathing deeply and slowly.
- Rub your hands together to get the blood flowing.
- Make a fist with one hand and use it to tap gently down your arm.
- Repeat on the other arm.

Pressure points

These should be applied in this order on both sides of the body. As you apply pressure, keep the hand not applying pressure on your horse's body to feel for muscles twitching. Pay attention to relaxation responses (i.e., licking, chewing, yawning, lowering the head).

Shen men

- This is also referred to as heart 7.
- This clears the brain and calms the horse.
- It's located on the outside of the front leg, just above the knee/carpus bone towards the back of the leg.
- Apply steady, gentle pressure with your thumb for 30 seconds.

Nei guan

- This point helps bond your horse to you.
- It allows your horse to relax and build trust in you by clearing the mind and promoting whole-body energy flow.
- It's referred to as pericardium 6.
- This point is located at the front of the chestnut, in the middle of the leg.
- Apply steady, gentle pressure with your thumb for 30 seconds.

Heaven's gate

- This point is common to most vertebrate animals.
- Look for the point at the connecting point between the lower back and the sacrum.
- It will feel spongy and not have any bone sticking up.
- Horses often groom each other in this area to relieve stress.

- Apply pressure here for 30 seconds, then release. Repeat.

Craniosacral therapy

Craniosacral therapy (CST) was originally developed by an osteopath who detected a third "pulse" in the body (similar to a heartbeat and breathing). Dr. William Sutherland hypothesized that the "stitches" that appear to hold the bones of the skull together allow the bones to flex, and this flowing third pulse affects the motion of all of the bones, tissues, and fluids from head to tail along the spine. This includes not only the cranium but also the cerebrospinal fluid, the central nervous system, and the sacrum.

When the flow of this pulse is blocked by stress, trauma, or normal aging, a horse can display physical or behavioral symptoms that indicate an imbalance that CST might help. These symptoms include:

- *Stall vices (i.e., cribbing, weaving, head shaking)*
- *Spookiness*
- *Tripping*
- *Trouble with the bit*
- *Tail wringing*
- *Tightness and tension along the spine*
- *Temporomandibular joint disorder (a.k.a. TMJ or TMD)*
- *Blocked (or excessively leaky) tear ducts*

A qualified practitioner can teach you simple techniques to help release a blocked pulse, but it is best to have them treated by a professional first.

BEMER

BEMER stands for Bio-Electromagnetic Energy Regulation. BEMER devices (blankets, wraps, etc.) use a pulsed electromagnetic field (PEMF) that sends targeted signals to areas where poor circulation or wound healing could use a boost.

If healing your horse by placing a wrap around a sore ankle or throwing a pulsing blanket over their backs sounds too good to be true, prepare to be astonished. There is a growing body of research that suggests that BEMER therapy can:

- Significantly improve lower back pain in horses
- Increase relaxation and recovery after exercise (as measured by heart rate and blood pressure)
- Improve local circulation to speed healing
- Provide general improvements in tension and release

BEMER blankets and wraps are not cheap. A blanket costs $4500 or more, with used ones slightly cheaper (not sold by BEMER or covered by a warranty). It's best to locate an equine bodyworker skilled in this type of therapy.

Massage

Massage might be the one bodywork technique that even the most inexperienced horse owners are familiar with, most likely because techniques are similar to those used on humans.

There are many different forms of massage, but the main goals are the same: to increase blood flow to muscle tissues, to loosen muscle tightness, and to speed healing. A side benefit of massage is that many horses find it deeply relaxing.

If you want to treat your horse to a relaxing massage from head to tail, try these simple techniques. Make sure to move slowly, and repeat on both sides.

Neck

Make a loose fist. Use the back of your fingers in that loose fist to trace a line along the bed of the mane and down the front of the shoulder. Repeat three to five times.

Mane bed

Some horses love this — others can't stand it. Place your hands next to each other over the mane at the withers. Apply a gentle squeeze as you move the mane bed gently back and forth (like you are wringing out a washcloth). Move up to the poll and back down if your horse enjoys this.

Shoulder

Make a loose fist. Again use the back of your fingers to move from the top of the shoulder down toward the ground. Do this all across the shoulder blade.

Front of the chest

Using a loose fist, press firmly into the base of the neck on the horse's chest, and move slowly down. Be mindful with this — some horses are very sore in this area. Adjust your pressure accordingly.

Back

Use a flat hand and firm pressure to sweep from the withers along the side of the spine, about two inches down from the actual spine, all the way to the space between the croup and the point of the hip. This should be reasonably firm, but gauge your horse's response and adjust. Repeat three times.

If your horse enjoys this, switch to the heel of your hand and repeat the movement, adding pressure to really get into the muscle. This can be repeated five to ten times.

Hind

Start with the same flat hand that you used on the back. Start with lighter pressure at the croup and sweep down the buttocks using multiple strokes.

Next, use your fingertips to go against the muscle. Start at the point of the hip, and press with the fingertips first to the top of the buttocks (up), then down. It's a motion like scrubbing a floor, moving across the muscles. Repeat this along the entire upper portion of the buttocks once or twice.

If your horse is sore, they may tuck their hind under to avoid this. Move more lightly, or skip this altogether.

Next, use the heel of your hand to press small circles across the entire hind. This breaks stiff muscles up even further.

Note that some people use a hand massager on the glutes, but when starting out using your hands allows you to better gauge any tightness and be more connected to your horse's response.

Hamstrings

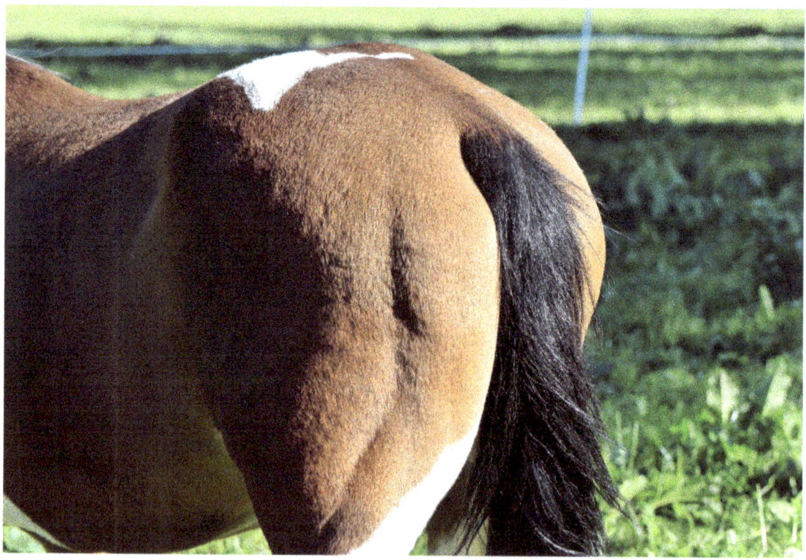

Many horses are very sensitive in their hamstrings. If they dance around, kick out, or avoid touch in this area, use appropriate pressure and stay in a safe position. If you are uncomfortable with their response, trying another type of bodywork may be best.

For horses who accept this type of massage, use the same techniques you used on the back and glutes. With a flat hand and pressure, sweep down the length of the hamstring a few times.

Next, use the fingertips of one hand to run across the hamstrings from just inside the leg under the tail towards you down the hamstring. Repeat five or ten times, increasing pressure to loosen the hamstrings further as your horse's muscles warm up.

T-Touch

Linda Tellington-Jones created the T-Touch system of bodywork in 1978. Using prescribed circular movements all over the horse's body, this method:

1. Eases anxiety
2. Improves performance
3. Benefits general health
4. Creates relaxation in a horse's body and mind

The basic movement is easy to learn.

- Place your non-dominant hand on your horse to steady and connect with them.
- Imagining the face of a clock, place a slightly curved pointer finger at six o'clock.
- Place the thumb down for stability.
- Move your pointer finger one and a quarter clockwise circles.
- Press firmly enough that you move the skin (not just the hair).
- Make sure the circle you create is an actual circle.
- Move to another spot and repeat the circle.
- Spots can be random, or you can use a system (i.e., moving in parallel lines from the shoulder to the hind).

The circle is the basic method of touch, but deep work also includes lifting the legs and using your hands to slide across a horse's body to evaluate tension and reflexive adverse reactions.

Masterson Method®

The Masterson Method® uses a light touch and movement while your horse is relaxed to help them release accumulated tension and pain in the muscles and the fascia (connective tissue). The key to this method is paying close attention to how your horse responds and what their body feels like under your hands.

While it is impossible to explain all of the anatomical releases you can achieve with your horse using this method, here are two techniques that all horses can benefit from (and are an easy way to connect to your horse).

Shoulder release

- Stand by the horse's shoulder, facing forward.
- Lift the front foot nearest you, bending it and supporting it inside the fetlock joint and at the knee.
- Wait for your horse to relax and release the shoulder.
- Lower the foot with the hand at the fetlock joint while using the other hand to straighten the knee.
- Place the foot down so that the whole leg stretches back, with the foot flat on the ground.
- Step back and let him relax into the shoulder opener.
- Repeat on the other side.

Lateral cervical flexion

- This releases tension in the poll, which then releases tension in the body.
- Stand at the left shoulder.

- Place your left hand on your horse's nose.
- Place the right hand four inches below and behind their left ear (this point is called the atlas).
- Gently flex the head towards you as you apply gentle pressure on the atlas.
- You are not forcing the head towards you — you are asking your horse to release the tension in the poll so they can relax.
- Once they show signs of relaxation (licking, chewing, or a feeling of softness under your hand), release both hands slightly, then move your right hand down the spine two or three inches, and ask for flexion again.
- Wait for a release, then slightly relax the pressure, move your right hand another two or three inches down, and ask for flexion.
- Repeat this until you've moved all the way down the neck and the horse's head is at the shoulder (this may take time and multiple sessions for stiff horses).
- Do not force movement at any time.
- If your horse fidgets or pulls away, do not increase pressure, but stay with them. This often means they are ready to release.

SURE FOOT pads

SURE FOOT pads are a simple way to help your horse relax and retrain the muscles they use for balance simultaneously. How? Pads vary in hardness from soft to firm. When your horse steps on them, they will give slightly, forcing your horse to pay attention to what's going on underneath their feet.

Equine balance pads are great for helping trail horses learn to pay attention to where they are stepping. They are also build proprioception (body awareness) and stability along the balancing muscles of the horse's body. Even with the subtle changes in balance, many horses find these very restful.

Using this tool is simple and works best in an area where your horse feels comfortable and relaxed. Avoid places and situations that would not allow them to stand quietly.

- On level ground, lift one foot at a time and place it on the pad.
- Pay attention to your horse's reaction as they step on the pad. Give them time to adjust to the sensation of the pad under their foot before asking them to lift another foot and step onto another pad.
- Let your horse rest on the pads until they step off.

Because you are training muscles that may not be strong, limit the use of equine balancing pads to two or three times a week. Once the stability muscles become stronger, they can be used more frequently (or as needed to maintain fitness and balance).

Lymphatic drainage

The lymph system in horses (and humans) functions as a sort of channel that recirculates white blood cells either through the lymph nodes in specific points of the body or out of the body through the urinary tract. It keeps the horse's fluid levels balanced and bolsters the immune system to prevent infection and keep your horse healthy.

Movement allows lymph to flow throughout the body, but even in horses with ample turnout and exercise lymphatic drainage can become slow or blocked. Some horses experience swelling in the legs when this occurs, but they may also be sluggish, stiff, and reluctant to move out.

Although lymph can be found deep in the body, lymphatic drainage uses a light, pumping action to stimulate flow in lymph beneath the skin. Your touch should be light but not irritating — this should be relaxing for your horse. There are specific techniques for specific areas of the body, but for general improvement in lymphatic flow, follow this sequence of movements.

- Start with both hands spread wide and placed on the side of your horse just above the heart.
- Apply a light downward movement toward the heart - think gentle pumping or tugging of the skin toward the heart. Do this movement twice, then pick up your hands and place them a couple of inches higher (toward the withers).
- Pump downward twice.
- Once you get to the withers, reverse course and keep tugging gently until you get back to where you started.
- Begin to move up the neck, fingers spread wide and toward the poll, stretching the skin lightly down as you go.
- If your horse tolerates it, you can gently tug on the cheeks, down the side of the nose, and under the chin.
- Reverse course, tugging gently as your move back down to the heart.

This movement stays the same as you move down the barrel and back to the heart, then down the side of the spine and back. You can then proceed to each leg, wrapping your hands around the leg so the fingers are inside the legs, then tugging gently up (toward the heart) while moving the hands down the leg and back up.

Using both hands and keeping the pumping action rhythmic and predictable is also key. This is gentle enough to use around healing injuries and tissues, but the rhythm keeps it easy for your horse to lean into with less stress.

Most horses find this deeply relaxing and will cock a leg and go to sleep. However, horses that have injuries or pain in their body may not enjoy a full-body session. Start slow and add on if it's clear your horse enjoys it.

Myofascial release

Myofascial release is frequently mislabeled as a deep-tissue massage technique.

Understanding what fascia is and how it can impact your horse's movement and overall comfort is important.

Fascia is connective tissue made up mainly of collagen and water. It not only encases the muscles (think of that silvery membrane on the outside of a chicken breast); it also weaves into the muscle itself and gathers to form tendons and ligaments. Some researchers believe that bones themselves are hardened connective tissue.

Because it weaves throughout the entire body, tight fascia in one part of the body can affect another part. Tight, restricted fascia can lead to a variety of problems, including:

- Difficulty with balance
- Poor or no collection
- Inflexibility
- Challenges with lead changes
- Dragging feet
- Acting "girthy" or "cinchy"
- Grumpy behavior
- Back pain
- Sore muscles
- Swelling in the tendons and ligaments
- Increased injury
- Sore muscles
- Overall poor attitude

But it's impossible to complete a simple massage to release this tension. Fascia — wrapped around muscles or in the form of tendons and ligaments — cannot be manipulated in short, sharp bursts. It only releases, stretches, and softens with steady pressure applied for a longer period.

With time, this release:

1. Improves range of motion
2. Deepens flexible
3. Supples your horse
4. Improves movements
5. Improves attitude
6. Relieves pain
7. Relaxes your horse

Although nothing beats a full myofascial release session with a qualified practitioner, there are some points on your horse that you can manipulate for a general release. It's important to keep an eye on your horse's response. Look for licking, chewing, softening, and relaxing.

Use this simple technique to relieve myofascial tightness at the poll that causes pain in the face and jaw.

- Stand just in front of the horse's shoulder, facing the same direction.
- Loop two loose fingers under the cheekpiece of the halter (you're not gripping or pulling).
- Have a treat in the hand not on the halter. Place the treat under the horse's chin (they should know it's there).
- As they reach for the treat, bring it back toward their chest so they stretch into their poll.
- Hold for a few seconds, then release.
- You can give the treat or not.

Tension in either side of the neck can also cause pain and tension in the jaw, head, and face. To release it:

- Stand next to your horse's shoulder, facing the same direction.
- Run your fingers down the side of the neck, locating what feels like regular

"hills and valleys" that follow the bones of the neck. These slight depressions are where you'll add pressure.

- Stagger your feet to get a strong foundation for yourself (almost like you'll be in a lunge).
- Place the hand closest to your horse on a valley that is mid-neck (about a handprint away from your horse's jaw).
- Have a treat in your other hand.
- Take a deep breath, and on an exhale, press firmly into the valley with the heel of your hand as you show your horse the treat and ask him to bend his neck toward it. Depending on your horse, you'll hold this for five to 30 seconds.
- Inhale to release, straightening his head as you do, move down to the next valley, then press firmly into the next valley, asking for flexion as you do with the treat.

Next, move to the engine of your horse and the origin of many instances of fascial tightness: the hindquarters. For this, you can use a smooth tool designed for this purpose (a gua sha stone), or use the heel of your hand, the side of a fist, or the smooth lid of a jar.

- Locate the highest point of the hip, then move about eight inches toward the horse's head.

- Avoiding the bone and staying on the muscle, use the tool or your hand to press and sweep from that starting point to the highest point on the hip.
- Don't be shy about pressure — you'll need to make it firm to release the fascia. Do pay attention to your horse, though, and adjust. You might start at one level of pressure, then go deeper as the horse begins to release.
- Sweep five to ten times. You'll repeat this on the other side.

To further release fascia in the hind end:

- Anchor the heel of your hand on the horse's hip bone.
- Keeping your heel steady, use your tool to sweep the muscle from the highest point (where you started in the last exercise), creating a quarter circle down the gluteal muscle.
- Sweep five to ten times. Keep checking in with your hand to feel the release of any tightness or knots.
- Repeat this on the other side

For additional release and relaxation, clasp your hands just above the hip bone to create a small ledge. With both elbows pointing straight down, apply downward pressure to open the sacrum and hips. Hold for ten to 30 seconds, then release. Repeat on the other side.

One final technique releases the hips and softens the glutes.

- Create a diamond shape with both hands.
- Place the diamond on the croup.
- Once the diamond shape is in place, press down through the fingertips for ten to 20 seconds. They will look like claws pressing into the area around the croup.
- Add a slight vibration to your fingers.
- Release.

Whole-body vibration

Whole-body vibration therapy was invented by Dr. John Harvey Kellogg (yes, the cereal maker) in 1895. In the 1960s, NASA explored the possibilities of this modality's healing powers, using it to counteract bone loss and muscle imbalances caused by long periods in zero gravity.

For horses, whole-body vibration is conducted by standing on a platform that vibrates between 30 and 50 Hz for 20 or 30 minutes at a time. Multiple studies have found significant benefits to this type of bodywork, including:

1. Improved back muscle development

2. Increased hoof growth

3. Faster tendon and ligament healing

4. Relief of stress and pain

While purchasing a whole-body vibration machine is possible, be prepared for sticker shock. These can be added to a stall floor for tens of thousands of dollars, or one of the smallest freestanding models will set you back at least $6,800. Many rehab centers use this technology, though, so if this sounds like something that would benefit your horse, search for qualified facilities in your area.

CONCLUSION

"Riding a horse is not a gentle hobby, to be picked up and laid down like a game of solitaire. It is a grand passion. It seizes a person whole and once it has done so, he will have to accept that his life will be radically changed." Ralph Waldo Emerson

Learning to bond with horses has been a winding road with many missteps. I have felt foolish, discouraged, ecstatic, joyful, angry, abundant, broke, peaceful, and secure — sometimes all on the same day.

But in the end, there is this: Hank, my crotchety introverted loner of a horse, the one who I "adopted" from an absentee owner at my lesson barn in 2021, the one who is known for his curmudgeonly ways and darting near-bites of pretty much every person or animal who gets too close.

When I took over his care, all I knew was he was "free" (and we all know how that goes), he had a few minor health complaints, and he was my regular lesson mount. I wanted to enter back into horse ownership after a horse-less decade, and he was convenient (if I'm honest. Love the one you're with!).

And so we started to really get to know each other. I visited him every day, sometimes to ride, sometimes to hang out in the pasture or get some bodywork done. I worked with his barn to fine-tune his nutrition to address (and mostly clear up) free fecal water syndrome. I soaked his abscessed foot and hung out with him through the three months of lameness that followed. In winter 2022, Hank received a borderline Cushings diagnosis, and I adjusted his diet once again.

Through it all, we were refining all of the suggestions in this book. We did groundwork, transferred it to the saddle, and tried to figure out how to get my elder equine friend into a canter I could actually sit. I updated his first aid kit (and mine) and evaluated and cleaned his tack and gear. I braided my own reins, then built trail obstacles for my barn and guided Hank through them, first on the ground and then under saddle.

And some days, all we did was take a hike through the beautiful Graham Area of the Gunpowder Falls State Park where Hank lives. We watched all four seasons cycle through as we navigated the trails, got better at water crossings, and watched a growing herd of dozens of deer bound away from us on one memorable hike. With me on foot and Hank lazily following behind, we watched a fox skulking around her den and foraged for wineberries, stinging nettle, and garlic mustard, hot summer sun blocked by a lush canopy of hardwoods and cooling breeze lifting Hank's mane and surfer-boy forelock and kissing the back of my neck.

I no longer go to the barn with an agenda other than to see Hank and enjoy his company. These days, instead of burying his head deeper into the round bale or walking off to lay down, Hank actually backs away from the round bale, turns to me, and stretches his head toward me, nose down, for the halter. His eyes are softer, his body is healthy, and, at 27 years old, he is in the best shape he has been in since I have known him. Other boarders and his lesson riders comment on the change — he is more relaxed, more enthusiastic, and sweeter. Now, he is interested in what we are doing, no longer shut down and just doing what he's told until it's over.

This is what it means to connect with horses. It's developing a partner, building a foundation of trust and respect with your horse so that you both get what you want. This helps balance your needs and goals with your horse — whether that's long-distance rides, leisurely hacks, or Grand Prix dressage — with your horse's need for stability, safety, and security. It's honoring them as a functioning individual with opinions, a sense of humor, and personality quirks that make them who they are.

"At its finest, rider and horse are joined not by tack, but by trust. Each is totally reliant upon the other. Each is the selfless guardian of the other's very well-being." Anonymous

This guardianship of our horse's well-being somehow turns into another way to care for ourselves — to look into the liquid mirror of our horse's eye and see our own beauty reflected within and without.

The connection is worth the time.

The bond is worth the effort.

The return on both is immeasurable.

Happy trails.

RESOURCES

The books below can take your further on your journey to building a better bond with your horse.

Acton, Lynn. *What Horses Really Want Unlocking the Secrets to Trust, Cooperation and Reliability*. North Pomfret, Vermont, Trafalgar Square Books, 2020.

Brannaman, Buck. *Groundwork*. 1997. Santa Ynez, California, 2017.

Desmond, Leslie, and Bill Dorrance. *True Horsemanship Through Feel*. Lyons Press, 20 May 2014.

Dorrance, Tom. *True Unity*. Milly Hunt Porter, 1987.

Eversole, Robert. *The ABCs of Trail Riding and Horse Camping*. 20 Oct. 2021.

Gore, Tom, et al. *Horse Owner's Veterinary Handbook*. Hoboken, N.J., Howell Book House/Wiley Pub, 2008.

Gosmeier, Ina. *Acupressure for Horses*. North Pomfret, Vermont, Trafalgar Square Books, 1 Aug. 2018.

Hill, Cherry. *101 Ground Training Exercises for Every Horse & Handler*. North Adams, Massachusetts, Storey Pub, 2012.

Hill, Cherry, and Richard Klimesh. *Horse Handling and Grooming : A Step-By-Step Photographic Guide to Mastering over 100 Horsekeeping Skills*. Pownal, Storey Publishing, LLC, 2012.

---. *Horse Health Care*. Storey Publishing, LLC, 22 July 2014.

Jones, PhD, Janet L. *Horse Brain, Human Brain: The Neuroscience of Horsemanship.* North Pomfret, Vermont, Trafalgar Square Books, 2020.

Masterson, Jim. *Beyond Horse Massage.* Trafalgar Square Publishing, 1 Nov. 2011.

Schöpe, Sigrid. Training and Riding with Cones and Poles. North Pomfret, Vermont, Trafalgar Square Books, 30 Oct. 2021.

Smith, Kristi, and Linda Parelli. *How to Develop Emotional Fitness in Horses*. Happy Horse, Happy Life, 2021.

Swift, Sally. *Centered Riding*. North Pomfret, Vt., Trafalgar Square Publishing, 1985.

Tellington-Jones, Linda. *Improve Your Horse's Well-Being*. North Pomfret, Vermont, Trafalgar Square Publishing, 1999.

PHOTO CREDITS

Thanks to all of the photographers who have contributed to this book with their work. Every picture in this book is provided without a requirement for citation, but I feel it's important to recognize the work of other artists. The photographer's name or internet handle (whichever they provided) is first, followed by the page on which their work appears.

Front Matter

Dane Kolbeck (iii), Pixabay (iv)

Introduction

Aaron Anz (vi) Julissa Helmuth (7)

Part I

Barbara Olsen (8), Melike Benli (11)

Chapter 1: Desensitizing

Los Muertos Cres (12), Rex Pickar (15), karolisalive (17), Felix Mittermeier (20), Len Kadan (23), David Stoecklin (27)

Chapter 2: The Six Basic Movements

bila_perla_otakay (28), Wikimedia (31), Sonja Rasche (37), Wikimedia (39), Suzannah Kolbeck (41)

Chapter 3: Combining Desensitizing And The Six Basic Movements

Sasha Maslova (42), marjayd (44), PROMA (47), Wikimedia (49), Adobe Stock (51), modfos (53), Andrea Piacquadio (57)

Chapter 4: At Liberty

Michael Anfang (58), vprotastchik (60), Alexander Dummer (63), Wallpaper Flare (66), Tom Schaeffer (69)

Part II: Riding

Kyle Mackie (70)

Chapter 5: Six Basic Movements Under Saddle

Kajetan Sumila (72), Gustavo Fring (74), DepositPhotos (76), Phillipe Oursel (81)

Chapter 6: Developing An Independent Seat

Arthouse Studio (82), Barbara Olsen (86), Barbara Olsen (89), Pezibear (91), Art Tower (92), Farmgirlmiriam (95)

Chapter 7: Transitions Between The Gaits

Tiffany Bumgardner (96), RD-Fotografie (98), Pezibear (100), Howard R. Wheeler (102), Ollie Craig (105)

Chapter 8: Riding Exercises

Laila Klinsmann (106), Jordan Bergendahl (108), Adobe Stock (109)

Chapter 9: Try Something New

Janosch Diggelman (116),CCO Public Domain (123), Christin Noelle (124), Snuffleupagus (126), Marion (128), dozornaya (129), Pixabay (133)

Part III: Keeping Your Horse Healthy

Boys in Bristol Photography (134), Castorly Stock (137)

Chapter 10: Stretching, Long Walks, And Exercise

gaspar zaldo (138), Daiga Ellaby (140), Pezibear (141), Stefanie Poepken (146), JR Bradbury (148), Accept 001 (149), Ollie Craig (153)

Chapter 11: Grooming

Creative Commons (154), Hi Form Australia (156), Adobe Stock (159), Kelly Forrister (161), Congerdesign (165), CCO Public Domain (168)

Chapter 12: Bodywork For Connection

Joanne O'Keefe (170), Tiana (173), Ralphs Fotos (178), Content Pixie (186), rh65rh (189)

Conclusion

Alejandro Novoa (190), Suzannah Kolbeck (193)

Resources

Michael Rojas (194), ykaiavu (197)

Photo Credits

my-roof (198)

Acknowledgments

Missi Köpf (202)

ACKNOWLEDGMENTS

It has been over a decade since the original draft of this book was started, different from what it is today. A simple list of 300+ things to do with a horse, written in a flurry one April as a challenge to myself to write for 30 days straight.

Today, I want to acknowledge the people who were there for the original and those who helped shepherd this new, stronger, and more focused version into being. For the original list, Save the Horses in Cumming, Georgia, started me on my path to adult horse ownership, and my late husband, Dane Kolbeck, said "yes" every time I wanted to add to our herd. Ed Dabney introduced me to the concept of natural horsemanship and showed me a better way to communicate.

To complete this new and much-improved version, the Maryland State Arts Council awarded me a Creativity Grant for research and writing time, and the Graham Equestrian Center in Glen Arm, Maryland, let me play with the ponies and carve out some trail obstacles to practice on. I am also grateful to have found the horsemanship of Buck Brannaman and his teacher, Ray Hunt. Striving for their kind of partnership with another creature is worth waking up for every morning. We always go together.

My greatest and most patient teachers will never know how much they have saved my life. Sadie, Toccoa, Jim, Hank, and Otis: I owe you a debt I can never repay.

And finally, I am grateful for Sicily, my daughter. The world is a better place for having you in it — horses have my heart, but you are the love of my life.

www.ingramcontent.com/pod-product-compliance
Ingram Content Group UK Ltd.
Pitfield, Milton Keynes, MK11 3LW, UK
UKHW021838270726
14058UKWH00002B/221